INTERPRETATION: The tech-
nique of interpretation is illustrated by a sentence-by-

• To make more effective use
of language--the b?
day medium
--a

SENTENCE COMPLETION

Publication Number 230

AMERICAN LECTURE SERIES®

A Monograph in

The BANNERSTONE DIVISION *of*

AMERICAN LECTURES IN PSYCHOLOGY

Edited by

MOLLY HARROWER, Ph.D.

Research and Consulting Psychologist
New York, New York

SENTENCE COMPLETION

—A Projective Method for the Study of Personality—

By

JAMES QUINTER HOLSOPPLE

Division of Clinical Psychology
Psychiatry and Neurology Service
Department of Medicine and Surgery
Veterans Administration
Washington, D. C.

and

FLORENCE R. MIALE

Graduate Faculty of Political and Social Science
The New School for Social Research
New York, New York

CHARLES C THOMAS · PUBLISHER
Springfield · Illinois · U.S.A.

CHARLES C THOMAS · PUBLISHER
BANNERSTONE HOUSE
301-327 East Lawrence Avenue, Springfield, Illinois, U.S.A.

Published simultaneously in the British Commonwealth of Nations by
BLACKWELL SCIENTIFIC PUBLICATIONS, LTD., OXFORD, ENGLAND

Published simultaneously in Canada by
THE RYERSON PRESS, TORONTO

Library of Congress Catalog Card Number: 54-8129

Printed in the United States of America

To the Memory of

Knight Dunlap and of Hermann Rorschach

FOREWORD

IF YOU LOOK at a map showing the coastline of a rich but undeveloped country, you are likely to note numerous lines of communication running in from the coast, but none of them getting very far. So, near the beginning of this century, were the basic projective techniques that we know today. People were telling what they saw in ink-blots, what pictures meant to them, filling in gaps in sentences. But there was very little realization of these techniques as having psychodynamic meanings. They had not penetrated far enough inland, or fanned out laterally, to say nothing of vertically, to yield the multidimensional communications network that exists between them today, and to which they owe much of their significance. It is worth reflecting a moment on the fact that each of these techniques began its career as a means of assessing intellectual functions, without apperception of dynamic connotations until much later. Because the early understanding of these dynamic potentialities came mostly through the word-association test, we can forget that it too was long studied intellectualistically; one has only to examine the elaborate classificatory systems of its earlier development. As yet the history of psychology promises no more fascinating chapter than the account of how and why we then understood, or valued, so differently what we were already holding in our hands. About 1910 the writer of this foreword devised and briefly used, in substantial dynamic innocence, a series of phrase-completions that might have passed with a student of that time, as an alternate form of the series that this monograph offers us. But the lateral communications with the dynamic psychology of that day were too difficult for the procedure to make its way there. The word-association studies of Jung seem to have been those that definitively lifted projective functions from the intellectualistic to the dynamic level, and for this general process there is a major indebtedness to psychoanalysis. Indeed before that time it was not wholly respectable for a projective procedure to be psychodynamic; witness the stepchild history of handwriting, which only after allied procedures have reached status, is beginning to find a reluctant acceptance. (I am so far sympathetic that since the authors give us the choice, I should plump heavily for written responses to some at least of their incomplete sentences. Once on the dynamic level there are two possible developments, or stages of development. One of them emphasizes personality type or form, the other emphasizes psychogenic content. The word-association procedure has the most distinct history along both lines. But although still very *efficient,* word-association has not proved sufficiently *effective* to maintain itself as a typological procedure beside the Rorschach, or as a content procedure beside Thematic Apperception. The function of sentence completion is to retain the efficiency of the old word-association, but greatly to improve on its effectiveness in the amount of information it makes possible. Like its ancestor, it is capable of same-order contributions in areas of typology and of dynamic content.

Critical observers do not seem to rate highly the validity of any projective method, as method. Certainly the present authors make no such claims for Sentence Completion. It is a question of what you, as a user, can make of the method. These authors have, with freely expressed purpose, discouraged the user who depends much on predigested formulae of any sort. They lay more stress on talent in the examiner; his capacities for sympathy and empathy. They are optimistic about ease of acquiring the method, with justice, one hopes. But it makes the intellectual demands on qualities said to be needed by the successful cryptanalyst: wealth of imaginative power; exceptional capacity for close, sustained application, and for back-and-forth reasoning between abstract and concrete. "Sharp and powerful" in the authors' phrase, Sentence Completion suggests rather those legendary weapons which are resistless when valiantly wielded, but turn again to smite and shame those who bear them unworthily. In personal conversation, the most critical judge in the field I know, rated the sentence completion procedure as the foremost of the psychodiagnostic techniques; but on that account it could the more mislead you and those you counselled, if you used it rashly or imperceptively. The aim of this volume is that Sentence Completion shall serve the psychodiagnostician well. May the insights of all users make the best of both.

FREDERICK L. WELLS

ACKNOWLEDGMENTS

I‌T IS NOT possible to list or even to remember all of the persons to whom we are grateful for completing either our incomplete sentences or our incomplete thoughts during the last six years. We are especially indebted for significant contributions to Sara Barin, Inge Bogner, Barbara Bowen, Nell Holsopple, H. M. Houtchens, R. L. Jenkins, Camilla Kemple, Maurice Lorr, George Miale, Lucretia Pile, Jane Schick, Maethel Shindelman, and J. M. Stauffacher.

J. Q. H.
F. R. M.

CONTENTS

(xiii)

SENTENCE COMPLETION

No. 73. TESTS LIKE THIS

" 'Twas brillig, and the slithy toves
Did gyre and gimble in the wabe;
All mimsy were the borogoves,
And the mome raths outgrabe."

". . . . 'There's glory for you,' said Humpty Dumpty. 'I
don't know what you mean by glory,' Alice said. . . . 'Of
course you don't—till I tell you. I meant "there's a nice knock-
down argument for you." 'But glory doesn't mean a nice
knockdown argument,' Alice objected. 'When I use a word,'
Humpty Dumpty said in rather a scornful tone, 'it means just
what I choose it to mean—neither more nor less.' "

Obviously in this colloquy Lewis Carroll is casting Humpty
Dumpty in the role of examiner and Alice in the role of respondent.

" 'The question is,' said Alice, 'whether you can make words
mean so many different things,' 'The question is,' said Humpty
Dumpty, 'which is to be master—that's all. . . . They've a
temper, some of them—particularly verbs, they're the proudest—
adjectives you can do anything with, but not verbs—however,
I can manage the whole lot of them.'

" 'You seem very clever at explaining words, sir,' said Alice.
'Would you kindly tell me the meaning of—' "

But unfortunately Lewis Carroll had not heard of the modern
sorcery of diagnosing another's personality when he interrupts
you and completes a sentence you had started.

BENJAMIN'S POSTSCRIPT. SEE PAGE 73.

The psychologist is by no means alone in recognizing that the flexibility of language may serve either to make self-revelation possible or
to render an interpreter more secure in his misinterpretation. Benjamin,
a subject whose complete record appears on pages 72 to 82, added the
above as a spontaneous postscript to his sentence completion, thereby
making his own position clear—an understandable position with which
the authors have considerable sympathy.

Chapter 1

PROJECTIVE USE OF INCOMPLETE SENTENCES

VERBAL ASSOCIATIONS to verbal stimuli have for decades occupied a central place in personality study and in the development of techniques of psychological analysis. Single word associations to single word stimuli have never been ideal material. The responses are too staccato, the full meanings are too difficult to grasp. On the other hand, free associations to constantly changing and unidentified stimuli, as in the analytic procedure, or in unstructured interviews, do not provide the examiner with a stable background from which to draw his inferences. Sentence completion, lying midway between these two techniques, offers an almost ideal compromise. Furthermore, by giving a subject an opportunity to reveal himself without committing himself, the sentence completion may be constructed to meet the primary requirements of the projective method. The individual may be permitted to behave in a way which is altogether characteristic of him and consistent with the structure of his whole personality.

One of the serious limitations of the more widely used projective tests, which seems not to handicap sentence completion, has been the extensive technical training required for competence in their application. Rorschach interpretation requires of the clinician, besides broad and deep clinical knowledge and experience, a thoroughgoing acquaintance with what amounts to a whole new language, and years of experience with it are required to gain facility in translating the language of wholes and details, color and shading and movement, into meaningful descriptive English. Although sentence completion technique clearly offers much promise in overcoming this limitation, neither the kinds of sentence openings used, nor the techniques of interpretation, have hitherto permitted anything approaching full use of sentence completion as projective material. Sentence completion tests have usually approached the individual too directly. They have asked for a conscious report on problems, and therefore attacked and exposed the subject. The subject's conscious attitudes have masked the material from which valid inferences concerning more or less unconscious trends could be drawn.

Our material consists of 73 incomplete sentences, which seem to call for relatively impersonal responses, rather than for report on personal problems. Administration may be oral or written, individual or group. Although the procedure is not lengthy, there is no time limit. The present form has developed through eight mimeographed versions. More than 1,700 individual records in one edition or another have contributed the data from which our criteria for inclusion, exclusion, and modification of sentences have emerged. Records were obtained from patients in mental, tuberculosis, and general medical and surgical hospitals, in outpatient clinics, from private patients referred by psychiatrists, from a state prison and a home for the aged, from college students, psychologists, physicians, office workers, student nurses, military personnel, normal and pathological family groups, and from the more docile among our friends, acquaintances and relatives.

Like other projective methods, this one is no substitute for clinical experience. However, competent clinicians can begin to use it after a few hours' training. A major value, which lies in its use in a battery of projective methods, is shown perhaps most dramatically in many cases where Rorschach or TAT records are meager. It seems often to put flesh and blood on the structural picture obtained from other techniques, providing material which substantiates or clarifies very subtle indications from other techniques.

We do not think of this version as final. Items were originally considered for many reasons, and the content was derived from many sources. The Tendler, Rohde, Office of Strategic Services, and University of Michigan tests all contributed something to our thinking. Some items were originally chosen with the hope, now abandoned, that they would throw light on a particular aspect of personality. Of these, some have retained their place, but more often than not because of their utility in unexpected connections. For many items, the only criterion of selection which can now be identified is that they seemed to be a good idea at the time, and we suspect that some of them remained in the series because we liked them. Certain of the openings now included will surely be omitted later. Better ones will be substituted. We do not seek to freeze the instrument in its present form but rather to provide a good series of openings which can be improved on a rational basis.

As noted above, the procedure may be either oral or written. It is not possible to say at this time which procedure is better. Indeed, further experiment will be required to establish the precise differences resulting from alternative methods of administration. One point is clear. There is no special virtue in the instruction to respond rapidly. In fact, the reverse may be true. Spontaneous, quick responses seem to make use of the unconscious defense mechanisms of the subject more effectively than do responses which follow long deliberation. And the unconscious mechanisms are often more difficult to analyze than are the conscious. Until more definite evidence is available for differentiating between the effects of oral and written presentation, the choice appears to be best made on the bases of subject preference and examiner convenience.

The procedure in dealing with sentence completion data is a procedure of interpretation, and is not a procedure of scoring. The authors, no less than other psychologists, have had to contend with their own desire and suggestions from the outside that the endings to the sentences be examined sentence by sentence, in order that some value might be assigned to a particular ending with respect to a particular type of disorder or conflict. This desire to achieve a scoring system which would provide for a more "objective" handling of the data sounds like a reasonable desire, but we believe that an effort in this direction at the present time would be premature. Ultimately it is possible that a particular ending may be assigned to a particular syndrome, a particular conflict, a particular personality type, and that some scoring system may be devised which suggests that this individual belongs to this or that diagnostic group. For the time being, however, we believe that more and better material can be acquired by a process of interpretation sentence by sentence until an acceptable global description is achieved.

The extent to which the sentence completion as a projective technique meets present conventional formal requirements of test reliability and validity is a problem which now has no solution. Indeed, if we are correct in our belief that the examiner himself is an integral part of this instrument, the problem has no meaning unless the reliability and validity of the examiner component be known. It appears to us to be probable that with the sentence completion the examiner's essential role may be more effectively and directly studied than is the case with other projective techniques.

A large part of the difficulty in the matter of validity and reliability may stem from the historical accident that early mental tests and measurements were designed by psychologists whose education, training, and thinking were rooted in the physical sciences, and by biologically oriented psychologists who were overly impressed by the rapid strides in progress and invention being made by their colleagues in physics and chemistry. Thus the yardstick, the clock, and the scales, were taken not, as they should have been, as analogies for mental measurement, but as models which set the form and requirements for psychological instruments.

An alarm clock is not usually so reliable nor valid as a twenty-jewel watch, a tape measure is a less precise instrument than a set of calipers. The use of continua such as these for the comparison of instruments implies the essential equality of those who are making the measurements. For practical purposes in physical measurement, such equality can properly be assumed or by relatively simple training can easily be established. For only a few psychological procedures, and those of limited usefulness, is this true. For projective techniques it is not at all true because here the examiner is an integral part of the examining instrument itself.

Indeed, the "objectivity" of many psychological instruments has long been clearly, if quietly, recognized as illusory. For example, assuming the usefulness of the concept of "intelligence" and assuming it to be measurable, with the further assumptions that the tests will be given by clerks and scored by machines, there is an easily demonstrated actuarial superiority of one test over another. With an unlimited number of applicants for a job and a large number of selections to be made one may quite properly prefer the technique with the better batting average. But since the earliest days of intelligence testing it has been recognized that an experienced, competent psychologist with a relatively inferior instrument can arrive at a more dependable and useful judgment about a single person than can a stupid neophyte with the best of instruments. For projective techniques this is so clear as to need no discussion. The psychologist, then, who would use the sentence completion has two inseparable questions to answer. He must ascertain not only how valid and reliable is the test material, but also at the same time how valid and reliable is his use of it.

For the present we are forced to admit that neither age, professional status, academic training, years of clinical experience, nor professional affiliation provide values which can be written into a formula for determining how effective a particular psychologist will be in using sentence completion. Thus the responsibility at this point rests on the user to determine in accord with the best of his ethics and intelligence whether his conclusions deserve to carry weight. We have undertaken to provide a sharp and powerful tool. We cannot guarantee its skillful or constructive use. Fortunately, the user is not without resources. He can compare his inferences from the sentence completion alone with the judgments of wise persons who have known his subject long and intimately. And he can make predictions which can be checked by any observer.*

---

*No lack of concern on the part of the authors is responsible for omission of further discussion of interpreter validity. Although such discussion is admittedly complicated and difficult, we think there are better reasons for not going on with the matter in this monograph. We believe that no informed persons seriously question the ability of at least some psychologists to use projective material, including sentence completion, effectively. One current hypothesis is that skill and the ability to acquire it can be measured. Indeed, we would go so far as to argue that professional clinical psychology will not truly have come of age in modern society until such measurement is a matter of routine. We have no sympathy, however, with the position that if measurement of projective skill cannot be reduced to a quick, inexpensive, effortless, painless process, we can then afford to continue reliance on poor measurement, political certification, or no measurement at all. Adequate discussion here would be long and involved and would be tangential to our primary purpose—that of providing a skilful clinician with a usable tool. Furthermore, determination of how valid an interpreter may be can never be wholly separated from consideration (and possible modification) of the instrument which he uses. There would, then, in going into the matter be a natural inclination to modify or consider modifying the sentence completion procedure so that it would be maximally foolproof—that is, so that our less competent psychologists might make some productive use of the method. At this point such procedure is almost directly contradictory to our aim.

Chapter II

DEVELOPMENT OF THE
SENTENCE OPENINGS

Oᴜʀ ɢʀᴏᴜᴘ of incomplete sentences was developed through a most informal trial and error procedure. It was not systematically designed to conform with the structure of any established psychological theory, nor were criteria for construction, inclusion, exclusion, and modification of sentence openings firmly fixed in our own minds. However, certain guiding principles which were by no means clear at the outset can now be recognized as important in the development of the instrument.

Openings were selected to permit expression of thought or feeling with a minimum of threat or obvious exposure. Simple grammatical shifts from first to third person are clearly inadequate for this purpose. "He felt like killing himself when" is not an appreciable improvement on "I felt like killing myself when." In general thin disguises were avoided. Some protection against feelings of exposure is provided by the inclusion of openings which invite the use of clichés for completion.

Inasmuch as it is rarely possible to predict when an opening will be threatening to a particular individual, our objective in this respect can never be fully realized, and subjects experience varying degrees of discomfort. However, because we have succeeded to a considerable degree in meeting this criterion, the net effect on many subjects, especially the unsophisticated, is one of some relief derived from this opportunity for relatively free expression. A minimum of unpleasant affect seems to result in increased production of useful material.

Sentence openings which attack or threaten tend to elicit at worst impenetrable evasions and at best no more than reports of conscious attitudes. It was not our purpose to design a substitute for direct inquiry about the subject's conscious attitudes toward things, people and events of which he is fully aware and which he is quite willing to discuss. Gentle and humane interview techniques are a sufficient protection against threat and exposure where the question and answer method itself is appropriate. Our objective was to obtain material from which we might draw valid inferences concerning unconscious and semiconscious desires, motives, conflicts, and systems of personality organization.

A second important criterion is the usefulness of an opening in eliciting a wide variety of individual responses and in providing maximum flexibility for the subject in his interpretation of the meaning of the opening. The properties of simple association make it inevitable that almost any opening will call forth a certain number of stereotyped completions. Whenever the opening seemed to have considerable value but almost always evoked a cliché response, it was retained only if it evoked a considerable variety of clichés. For example, a high proportion of completions for the item "When fire starts" are stereotyped. Among the frequent ones are "call the fire department," "put it out," "keep calm," "run," "walk, don't run, to the nearest exit." A sufficiently wide range of choice tends to insure that the cliché will approach in significance a unique response. Similar logic applies to superficial, evasive, and facetious completions. Although we did not set out deliberately to elicit such responses we have found that they provide sufficient cover for the subject and enough range and variety in their nature to constitute a rich source of useful data.

Flexibility of interpretation of the opening increases the freedom of the subject to respond to almost any particular opening in accord with the unique structure of his own personality and may thereby give the interpreter data on a crucial aspect of that personality at a great many points throughout the record. The individual schizophrenic selects for himself those openings which will best describe his own schizophrenia. No one can predict which ones he will use for this purpose. Our early discovery of the value of this criterion has precluded selection, arrangement, or construction of openings based upon textbook chapter headings, diagnostic categories, or conventional typologies. It is not reasonable, therefore, to ask, "From what particular sentences does one derive information about sex adjustment, hysterical patterns, or other specific points of interest?" If any of these are of great importance to the subject he is likely to provide the relevant data for inference early and often.

Adherence to the criterion of flexibility exacts two penalties—both, in our opinion, far offset by the advantages. One is that the central condition described by a particular subject may not fall easily into one or another predefined category. For example, the production of a particular manic-depressive patient in a manic phase may resemble an agitated depression record more closely than it resembles another manic record. Perhaps this disadvantage is offset by the possibility that with skill and experience new and more useful categories may be discovered. The other penalty for flexibility and variety is that data are accumulated which do not lend themselves easily to mechanical classification, machine handling, and scoring. If, however, as we believe, the most effective use of any projective technique requires an essential contribution from the interpreter himself, then the effort to put projective data on mechanical scoring devices is a wild goose chase. But even were this not so, the breadth, depth and specificity of inferences which can be drawn from the wider range of responses to flexible openings seem fully to offset all penalties.

A third criterion is that of apparent clarity and simplicity of language, which makes the task easier for the subject and results in more spontaneous response. To be sure, the clarity must be more apparent than real and there must be enough ambiguity to permit effective projective use of the material. Closely allied to simplicity is the need for content which is related to the experience and concerns of the subject. This is a goal which is difficult to reach, and unfortunately there are still in the current version some items which reflect more strongly the psychological notions of the authors than the interests of most subjects.

A fourth criterion concerns the degree of structure inherent in the opening and implied for the completion. Relatively unstructured openings usually, but not always, contribute to the meaningfulness of the response. The degree of structure finally chosen for each opening was based on a trial and error determination of the optimum. For example, "A large crowd is" was improved by dropping the "is," but "One's closest friends" became far more useful by adding "can." In certain cases an apparently firmer structure actually permits greater variation in response. For example, "A man can stop beating his wife only if," which seems highly structured, yields a wider variety of response than some of its less structured variants.

A fifth criterion involved agreement between the au-

thors and many of their colleagues concerning the inferences to be drawn from completions to each opening and
from groups of completions. Clinicians quite unfamiliar
with this particular technique frequently have shown a
high degree of similarity in their inferences from the same
data. Where dissimilarities of interpretation do occur
among experienced clinicians they are likely to be due to
differences in emphasis or in theoretical orientation.

A sixth criterion could sometimes be used and was given
almost total weight when it was applicable. Sentences
which contributed to interpretations that were in substantial agreement with facts about the subject unknown
to the interpreter before his analysis of the completions
were highly prized.

In general, openings were discarded if they yielded important data in relatively few cases. However, a few of
these were retained because they occasionally elicit responses which are succinct and almost complete descriptions of a central aspect of the personality, for example,
the sentence discussed later in the record of Abner, "The
most pleasant dreams/are of fantasy and flattery." Sometimes the failure of a person to give an almost universal
response seems to be important. An additional value of
otherwise unproductive sentences lies in their contribution
to the total length of the task. When only those openings
are included which most often yield important data, the
task becomes briefer but the value of particular responses
diminishes. Thus we learned from one edition in which
only the twenty-five most often valuable openings were
used that many of the twenty-five distinctly lost utility.
The subject acts as if the inclusion of noncommital, unimportant completions permits him greater latitude in
responding to openings of high importance. For reasons
which have been stated, and particularly because of the

desirability of wording which combines simplicity of statement with strong emotional connotations, we find the words we have chosen derived frequently from the Anglo-Saxon, rather than from the Norman-French.

In summary, the openings which deserve a place in sentence completion are those which: threaten least and expose least obviously; permit variety of expression and flexibility of interpretation; lie within the experience and understanding of the subject; are relatively unstructured; invite completions which can be interpreted similarly by different clinicians; and invite completions from which the inference drawn can be checked against external fact.

Chapter III

CHARACTERISTIC COMPLETIONS

THE RANGE and variety of responses one is likely to encounter may be inferred from the following lists which contain for each sentence samples of completions which have been noted frequently or with special interest. In no case does a list constitute a completely adequate basis for a classificatory system of endings for that sentence. However, we have tried to indicate enough directions in which a respondent's thinking might go to insure that an examiner will feel some familiarity with the great majority of responses which he will be called upon to evaluate.

Many of the endings given take on varying, and often quite different, meaning, depending upon the way in which they are phrased.

a. The completion may be positive or negative, for example, *Compared with dogs cats are* "good house-pets," or "poor house-pets."

b. The sentence may be completed with "is," "should be," "can be," " or "may be," For example, *A naked man* "is" or "may be" cold.

c. The role of the subject of the completed sentence may be active or passive, for example, *When a criminal leaves a prison he* "goes straight," or "has been taught a lesson."

d. The completion may be in the imperative or the simple declarative, for example, *When fire starts* "run" or "everybody runs."

e. The time may be oriented to the present, past or future, for example, *A large crowd* "gathers," "gathered," or "will gather."

f. Obvious differences are noted in the identification of persons completing a sentence with one or another of the roles which may be implied in the same completion, for example, *The nicest thing about being a child* "is they have no worries," "you get candy."

g. There are considerable differences noted in the whole-hearted commitment of the person to the completion which he gives, for example, *A woman's body* "is beautiful," "is sometimes beautiful, and sometimes not."

h. There are marked differences in the definiteness and vagueness of responses which appear to be substantially similar, for example, *It hurts when* "you are wounded," or "you cut your finger."

i. There is wide variation in the amount of verbalization given in any particular response, for example, *When fire starts* "call the fire department" as compared with "self preservation being the first law of nature, try to send an alarm to fire headquarters."

In some instances the ending approximates one of those illustrated but varies in that the opening itself is changed by the respondent before completion. In such cases one is inclined to speculate on what the ending might have been had the opening been accepted as given.

1. *Children are usually certain that:*

They are loved; their parents love them, are perfect, good, right, unfair, will punish them; they are right, wrong; they are fed, hungry; they will get what they want, have their own way, get away with anything; they will grow up, grow up to be famous; things will turn out all right, they will be happy; they like to play; they have fun, have a good time, get ice cream, candy; there is a God; there is a Santa Claus, bogeyman, fairies; they must go to school, be obedient, do what they're told; life is their oyster; candy is good; what interest them interests others; parents are good for them but not to them; circuses are more fun than Sunday school; their parents have more privileges than they have; they must cross the street on the green light.

2. *People are praised when:*

They do a good job, do well; they do something exceptional; they do good, are helpful; they please others, do what others like; they deserve it; someone wants a favor, it is to the advantage of the one who praises; they try hard; they have something desirable; others happen to think of it; they do something others would like to be able to do; sometimes when they don't deserve it; they least expect it; they do something brave; you like what they do.

3. *A large crowd:*

Gathers; watches a game, parade, movies; is noisy, dangerous, hard to control; gathers quickly around an accident; is hard to get through; gathers fast; is a pain in the neck; wandered outside; are always in the N. Y. subways; is easily swayed; can easily consist of three persons two lovers and a chaperone; can mean disaster if a fire breaks out; is too many people, is something I avoid whenever possible.

4. *A person is most helpless when:*

Sick, injured; paralyzed, crippled, blind; asleep,

unconscious; dead; drunk, drugged; threatened, frightened, in danger; restricted, his hands are tied, bound hand and foot; circumstances are against him; in bed, on his back; very young, very old; uncertain, doesn't know, lacks confidence, under strain, depressed; broke; sympathized with; cannot do things for himself; caught with his pants down.

5. *When an animal is wild:*

It is dangerous; it is free, independent, happy; people should be cautious; it is ferocious, fierce; it should be avoided; it is untamed, untrained; it should be caged; it is frightening; it is hard to handle, hard to tame; it lacks control; he ought to be shot; it runs out of its cage; a lot of times he harms other animals; it is afraid of humans; one should treat him gently; he should be avoided or tamed; one should not attack it or pet it; it is elusive; he is more beautiful; it usually dies an accidental death.

6. *The hardest decisions:*

Involve other people, those we love, family, oneself; are, are not the most important; require much, little, effort, time; are about money, marriage, the future, children; are made when you haven't enough knowledge; how to get along with the boss; between love and duty; I have to make; we can't agree on; are made by Congress; are made in the morning; are between two evils, those which hurt ourselves.

7. *The easiest way to get money:*

Work for it, earn it; steal it, take it, cheat, lie; win it, be lucky; inherit it; find it, marry it, have someone give it to you, borrow; save; invest, buy cheap and sell dear; invent something people want; there is no easy way; be a politician; go to the bank; keep sponging off my girl.

8. *Twenty years from now:*

I'll be 42; it will be 1974; the world will be better, worse; I will be married, have a family, money; I will be old, dead; there will be great technological advance, war, peace; who knows; what will I be doing; comes the revolution; I can retire; I won't have to take tests like this.

9. *Parents would worry less if:*

They trained their children better; they watched their children more carefully; they knew where their children were, they understood their children better; they were better adjusted, more secure; they trusted their children more, their children were brought up differently, their children obeyed; they were sure their children would not become sick; their children lived right; their children didn't stay out late; they had more money; they had less responsibility; they remembered their youth; children were adults; their children were shackled; they'd drop dead; they weren't human; their children were more aggressive against others; they used birth control; they were better educated, knew more about child psychology.

10. *When fire starts:*

Call the fire department, ring the fire alarm; put it out, put it out before it spreads; try to put it out; don't get panicky, people get panicky; it causes damage, the house burns; run, everybody runs; it must be kept under control; remain calm, don't lose your head; it burns, gets warm; get water, an extinguisher; there is always a crowd, people are there; help is needed; smoke rises; walk, don't run to the nearest exit; oxygen is rapidly taken from the atmosphere; fight it with fire; it must burn itself out; try to organize the situation mentally and act in an efficient manner; it spreads rapidly; try to put it out if it is destructive; fan it.

11. *Compared with dogs, cats are:*

Treacherous, sly, stealthy; sociable; docile, refractory; intelligent, stupid; quicker; quieter; friendly, unfriendly; feminine; independent; cleaner; the same; smaller; effeminate; nauseating; (a full list of completions for this sentence would approximate a full list of trait names).

12. *Fathers should learn that:*

Children are important, are people, have interests of their own; children grow up, can make decisions; children need love, tolerance, attention; they have responsibilities at home too; they can hurt, help their children; they should be kind, considerate; mother knows best, comes first; patience is a virtue; sons needs their companionship; wives have feelings too; what a nuisance motherhood is; they shouldn't get drunk; sons can be helpful; wives can be tolerant; it pays to be ignorant; there are limits to his dominance; their sons imitate them.

13. *One's closest friends can:*

Be helpful, trusted, counted on; do him wrong, hurt him, deceive him; lend him money; cause him embarrassment, annoy him; become one's enemies; get him a good date; foul him up; give one advice; be honestly critical; borrow things; be his father, mother, dog; be mad at him too.

14. *It is easy to get into trouble when:*

You look for it, ask for it, have a chip on your shoulder; you are careless, don't look before you leap, don't know what you're doing, act without thinking; drunk; angry; tired; exasperated; impetuous; you are disobedient, do something wrong, fool around with young girls; influenced by others, in bad company, you pal around with bums; one talks too much; one least expects it; you are helping somebody; you are not on guard; you are in a crowd; one is selfish, weak; one is ashamed to do what one thinks is right; strongly tempted; young; you have a distorted mind; no one cares; you don't understand.

15. *Few children fear:*

Their parents, mothers; death, life; animals (many varieties); the dark; financial problems; unless they are taught to; other children, their friends, smaller children; danger, evil, trouble; what is familiar, understood; the unknown, what is not understood; the future; love, truth, goodness; kindness; if they are secure; light, daylight; assuming responsibility, growing up; water; heights; music; dodos; food; butterflies; God; candy; fire; fear; their second Teddy bear; the thought of sleep; shadows; being treated wrong; me.

16. *At the end of the road:*

Is a field, house, gate, home, barn; fence, corner, sign, bridge; detour, turning, fork, another road; block, dead end; death, a graveyard; a ditch, precipice, ravine; a rainbow, a pot of gold; rest, resting place, peace; one stops, turns around; is a sign with complete instructions; a swimming pool, beach, picnic ground; let me live at the end of the road and be a friend to man; is where they found the body.

17. *He drew back from the touch of:*

Her hand; his hand; fire; the hot stove, iron, pot; the live wire; cold steel; cold water; slime; the sharp knife; the needle; the thistle; the beggar; the bore; death; success; the unknown; the cold, unclean, withered, hand; velvet; suede; fur; the mouse; the snake; the whip; the leper; the corpse.

18. *The white girl who married the colored man:*

Was brave, foolish, admirable, crazy, dumb, progressive; ostracized, outcast, humiliated, punished; disowned by her family; had a hard time; must have loved him, was driven by strong emotion; had her own ideas; didn't care what people thought; should be shot; lived happily ever after; didn't go on any honeymoon.

19. *The most pleasant dreams:*

Are of those you love, girls, home, money; are day dreams; wet dreams; rarely come true, end too soon, are rudely shattered, are only dreams; are ones in which you can be a hero, satisfy unfulfilled aspirations; are wish fulfillments; memories of the past, of dead people you loved; make you tired in the morning; are not remembered; have lots of color; happen in childhood; are exotic.

20. *A drunken man:*

Is disgusting, obnoxious, an ugly sight; is to be pitied, tragic; is uncontrolled, loses self control, is uninhibited; is unhappy, worries; is sick, mentally

sick; is helpless, dazed, loses his identity; is troublesome, annoys others; staggers, falls; is dangerous,
should be avoided; is foolish, a darn fool; is free,
happy; should be helped; arouses disgust and pity;
is sometimes funny, sometimes revolting; is a victim
of our society; should keep his drunkenness to himself; is a king in his own eyes; is seldom given pity;
is truthful; will sober up; is likely to get arrested;
gets a hangover; becomes amorous.

21. *No one can repair the damage caused by*:

Gossip, slander, rumor, ill will, injustice, thoughtlessness, malice, unkind words; fire, flood, storm,
earthquake, hurricane, war, atom bomb, fatal accident, disease; our own misdeeds, dissipation, yourself; carelessness, neglect; time; love, lack of love;
doctors who don't understand; Roosevelt, McCar-
thy; God—except God himself.

22. *The nicest thing about being a child:*

No responsibility, carefree, no worry; enjoyment of
novelty, freshness of experience; you grow up, the
prospect of growing up; you are taken care of, you
have security; the wholeheartedness; spontaneity;
being loved; innocence; naivete, ability to believe;
hope, optimism; lack of acquaintance with evil,
knowing only good; the opportunity to play; you
have fun, pleasure; being spoiled, the need to think
of no one but yourself; there isn't any; the sense of
endlessness; not being an adult; I can't recall; being
little; belief in Santa Claus; what's so nice about it;
you don't know what's going to happen; you can't
do wrong; not having to fill out tax returns.

23. *There is hardly any:*

Thing to do, sense in worrying, thing a person can't do if he tries; fun here, excitement; pleasure in evil; time to do what one wants; freedom in Russia, justice in a world divided; snow at the present time, air on a hot day, rain; meat on meatless days, thing to eat; thing left; uranium; fruit growing, fish in the water; Democrats left; way to do wrong, decency left in the world, fear of the devil; trouble today, trouble for me; need for poverty; space left; thing in a vacuum; good cops; boys left to play ball; body I dislike; persons in the world that don't make a mistake; truth in what she says; way to answer a sentence beginning 'there is hardly any.'

24. *To be without shame:*

Would be wonderful, is to be desired; is impossible, rare; is to be perfect, is sinful; a blessing, a crime; is good, bad, not too bad; is honor, to be without honor; is to have a clear conscience, be without conscience; is to be ignorant, crazy, abnormal, healthy, free; you should lead a good honest life; one should always live according to his conscience; is possible only for a small, healthy, happy child; is harder on the onlooker than on the shameless one; is possible only for someone beyond human frailty; you would have to be without blame.

25. *Worse than being lonely is:*

Being alone, stood up, no one to love you, without friends, forgotten, despised; hungry, broke, sick; depressed, bored, blue, miserable, heartbroken, sad, homesick, afraid, disturbed; away from your family; crowded; with someone you don't like; helpless, at sea, pushed around; in jail; in love; sick, dead; being alive; sober; having too much; having companionship and not being able to use it; afraid of suicide; fear of loneliness.

26. *When a person is ill:*

He needs help, understanding, sympathy; he needs a doctor, medical attention; he should go to bed, rest; he feels moody, depressed, grouchy, rejected, sorry for himself; he is irritating, annoying, stubborn; he wants to be alone, likes to be kept quiet; he will probably get better, probably die; he has a chance to relax; time is heavy on his hands; his perspective changes; he is unable to do his work properly; he is not mentally right; his cosmos, more than ever, is himself; it is better to do what he wishes.

27. *A man can stop beating his wife only if:*

He regains his senses, masters himself, changes his ways, realizes he is wrong, stops getting drunk, wants to; she is out, gives up, obeys him, leaves him, agrees with him, stops nagging; he loves her; he ever starts; he is stopped by the police; he receives treatment; she's dead; she beats him back; she pleads with him.

28. *The best thing about old age:*

Memories; wisdom; security; serenity, relaxation, peace; the satisfaction of having lived a good life; enjoying your children, the next generation; less work, obligations become fewer and fewer, your work is done; retirement; pension, social security; independence, companionship; nothing; one is able to do what one wants; dying; the end is near; the ardors of youth have subsided; you don't have to go off to war and have people worry about you.

29. *Children are most annoying when:*

They interfere with something you're trying to do; they make demands on you; they do things they shouldn't; they are poorly trained; you are tired, irritable; at a particular age; they are noisy; they are mischievous; they are angry; they are stubborn; crying; sick; awake; hungry; young; being spanked; beginning to get around; teething; spoiled.

30. *If people only knew how much:*

Generosity, good will, kindness, suffering, trouble, there is; better off they, the world would be if virtue, kindness, friendship, cooperation, the golden rule prevailed; they could help other people; people think of, like them; they don't know; more they could get out of life; they can do which is creative, valuable, useful; they bothered other people; better off than the next fellow they are; trouble there was in the world, they wouldn't complain about themselves so much; liberty costs; pain a little gossip may cause; I want; I like them; I need a wife; their appearance impressed others; good you were trying to do them and they didn't realize it; to say and when to say it; I feel let down at your sudden stop in the middle of that sentence.

31. *The main difference between a wild and tame animal is:*

Domesticity, training; freedom; friendliness, sociability; one will bite you, the other won't; its fear of you, your fear of it; the tame one can be kept on your property; gentleness, temper; they're different; the tame one learns tricks, is easier to train; the look in the eyes.

32. *Few things are less attractive than:*

A dirty, drunken, sloppy woman; death, dead people, animals; sickness, disease, accidents; a rat, skunk, snake, octopus; (sometimes read as "more attractive than" and completed accordingly: a beautiful woman; the forest in the fall.)

33. *The worst thing about being sick:*

Is you have to stay in bed; is being helpless; is the inactivity; is the pain, discomfort; is the loneliness; is being dependent on someone else; is the inability to meet responsibility, to get your work done; is the worry; is the dragging of time; is that other persons often have to suffer as well as yourself; is the confinement; would be if you couldn't think; that you can't tell them what's wrong with you; they can't treat you until they find out what's wrong; is the sickness itself; is that you have false sympathizers; is that you can get sicker; is that you're broke; is the way work piles up; is the loss of strength; is when no one cares to visit you; is the company one receives.

34. *It is often hard to sleep when:*

Worried, troubled, concerned with problems; excited, overstimulated; it is noisy, hot; ill; not tired, over-tired; one cannot relax; you are in strange surroundings; one has drunk coffee; one has an examination the next day; one leaves a project undone; one is confronted by a difficult decision; anyone nearby is snoring.

35. *People shouldn't:*

Gossip, talk too much; worry too much; drink too much, smoke too much; lie, criticize, be envious of others; do things which would injure themselves, bite their fingernails; make snap judgments, procrastinate; why shouldn't they; take baths in glass houses; expectorate in public; live forever; go without rubbers; believe all they hear; play with fire.

36. *To be a good liar one must:*

Practice, get experience; keep up his front, be consistent, be a good actor; have a good memory; have a good imagination; be careful; believe his own lies; have no conscience; be a heel, psychopath, politician, lawyer; tell the truth (sometimes with modifications); talk plenty; be cheerful; I never was a liar, I wouldn't know.

37. *A masculine woman should:*

Try to be more feminine, attractive, ladylike; try to tone down her masculinity; not be ashamed of her masculinity, act naturally, be herself; dress in a feminine way; dress accordingly, wear sports clothes; find a position to use her talents, work at a man's job; hide, keep out of sight; marry a feminine man; be psychoanalyzed, see a psychiatrist, be under a doctor's care; be sympathized with, not be made to feel uncomfortable; not have children; take a course on how to be a lady; be rich; find a congenial girl friend; be wondered about; use a depilatory; avoid me, for one thing.

38. *People refrain from murder only because:*

Of fear of the consequences; it is against the law; it isn't right, is immoral; they respect human life, each other; they can't, don't want to kill; it doesn't solve the problem; it is socially unacceptable; they can control themselves; the impulse is not strong enough to impel action; they like other people; its a horrible thing to do; of their inner feelings brought about by laws; they may tomorrow wish the victim were still alive; in our society it's just not practiced on a large scale; it is insane to murder anyone; of its effect inside them; they have strong super-egos; they are afraid of being punished, they're cowards; it isn't very nice to go around murdering people.

39. *Too much distance lies between:*

Washington and Moscow; New York and Paris; here and California; me and my friends; what I want and what I can do; my home and my old home; the earth and the moon; what people say and what they believe; birth and death; what is and what seems to be; theory and practice; children and their parents; home and business; people and the church; officers and men; dreams and reality; me and myself; the spoon and the mouth.

40. *The best of mothers may forget that:*

They were children, were young once; their children grow up; their children need their love, care; children are individuals, need to lead their own lives; they can be wrong, don't understand, don't know everything; she does not always know what is best for her child; their children love them; a child is a human being; the home comes first; their husbands need them; she has responsibilities; children are sensitive; children are not deliberately bad; everything she does is important to a child; their children have their own problems; her children are not only reflections of herself; equal love and affection should be showered on both children; one should not take oneself too seriously; silence is a virtue; children need a lot of rest; children should not be beaten; pop was in on the deal.

41. *There ought to be a law to:*

Prevent war, fires, murder; stop people from stealing; prevent gossip; stop jaywalking, speeding motorists; stop drinking; protect children, make men take care of families, educate parents, take care of old people; prevent interracial marriage, stop discrimination against minority groups; keep wages up; end all laws; eliminate crooked cops; reduce taxes; there are enough laws already; let people walk on the grass; outlaw quack psychologists; prohibit snoring.

42. *Spiders are:*

Insects, bugs; dangerous, poisonous; useful, industrious; spinners of webs; annoying, unpleasant; repulsive; harmless, rarely dangerous; arachnids; interesting; animals, creatures; not insects; creepy; fascinating to watch; weavers of exquisite webs; very dirty insects; leggy; good architects; found in damp cellars; our friends.

43. *When a criminal leaves the prison he:*

Goes free; is pardoned, paroled; is reformed; is happy; is anxious; goes somewhere else; reverts to crime, goes back to his old gang; is still dangerous; has a hard time ahead of him; has paid his debt to society; is marked, handicapped; doesn't always want to leave; gets $10 and a suit of clothes.

44. *Compared with sisters, brothers are:*

Stronger, bigger; rougher, bolder; better, worse company; much different, no different, about the same; males, masculine, more masculine; harder, easier to handle; closer, not as close; more, less, favored by their parents; more, less dependable; nice, wonderful; troublesome, bratty; teasers; more protective; I don't know, I never had a brother; less competitive if one is a girl; less considerate of parents; your right hand—buddy and companion; nothing but a cause of trouble.

45. *The finger pointed:*

At the accused, the guilty person, the criminal; at me, him, you; in the right direction; with scorn; at the wrong man; straight ahead, north, south, east, west; at the clock, the road, it; to the exit, the door, the window; to her disgrace; is bad manners; to the handwriting on the wall; to twelve midnight, at the little boy when the teacher said he was bad; at the dark doorway; menacingly, as the woman threatened and shouted.

46. *Children are least annoying when:*

Asleep, quiet; happy; playing; they behave, do what they are told; absorbed in anything, occupied with something; you are in a good mood, you like them; affectionate; unspoiled; well; they have a large room of their own; their true nature is appreciated; they reach the age of twenty-one.

47. *To avoid a fight one must:*

Control himself; use diplomacy, judgment, tact; make compromises; be strong; give in; run away; stop living; be tolerant of others; be clever; call the law; speak gently; try to be calm; I don't know how to avoid a fight; endure; be either a coward or forceful; give in a little bit; keep quiet; keep away from his enemies; hit first.

48. *A naked man:*

Has no clothes on, is nude, a nudist, is taking a bath; is cold; should get dressed; should be locked up; should not be on the street, was seen running down Broadway; is crazy, should be ashamed; looks foolish, feels silly; was swimming, enjoying himself, felt the goodness of the wind; would startle most women; is sometimes good looking; ran from the burning house.

49. *Closer and closer there comes:*

A day of reckoning; a time for decision; death; the end; self-control, independence, self-understanding; destiny, the turning point, the inevitable; age, old age; war, conflict, trouble; tomorrow, a day; examinations, income tax, graduation; world peace; success, career; inflation, depression, revolution, socialism; danger; the end of this test; a drunk, a train; a bird; the parade; spring; Christmas; one's next birthday; hope; dawn; night; the horizon; the hurricane.

50. *There would be more divorces if:*

The laws were less strict; there were less patience, understanding, tolerance, compromise; they were less expensive; it weren't for the social pressure, the stigma; they were easier to get; there were more marriages; the church weren't against them; more early, more hasty marriages; it weren't for the children; it weren't for the financial dependence of the wife; if people weren't too interested in getting

along with each other; there were less education;
there were more drinking.

51. *A drunken woman:*

Is immoral; loses control, is easily persuaded; is
stupid, foolish, disgusting; is a lot of fun, needs a
good man; is a disgrace, repulsive, sloppy, vulgar; is
worse than a drunken man, is the same as a drunken
man; might get hurt; is an object of pity; is a hog,
sot, no fit sight for children; degrades womanhood;
has a hell of a good time, may do a swan dive off a
bar; holds it better than a drunken man.

52. *When a person is wounded:*

He needs help, care, attention; you should call a
doctor; he bleeds; he is scared; he retreats; he is
sick, he suffers pain; he decides to act brave and
burden no one if possible; he should try to remain
calm until help arrives; he usually worries first
about how his loved ones would feel; it would be
best to leave; he hollers for help.

53. *One's best friend may be irritating when:*

He talks too much; he makes too many demands, is
selfish, possessive; he is in a bad mood, isn't feeling
well; one isn't feeling well, is ill, is tired; one wants
to be alone; one sees too much of him; he tells us
the truth about ourselves, points out your faults; he
gives too much advice; he is jealous; he wants to
borrow too much; he uses you for his selfish purposes; he does what you didn't expect him to do; he
disagrees with you; he persists in being obtuse.

54. *A woman's body:*

Is beautiful, is ugly, is sometimes nice; should be
soft, graceful; is an object of pleasure; needs cloth-

ing; has value; is sacred; is tender, frail; is her greatest asset; is dangerous; is different from a man's; is
expensive; shrinks with age; should be kept clean;
shakes; is wonderful to play with; was found in the
lake.

55. *A weak person does not often:*

Cause trouble; win battles; accomplish much; sur-
vive; take chances; get help; work; fight; make
friends; get around; have fun; live long; feel weak.

56. *Down underground:*

There are tunnels, subways, mines, natural resources, the remains of past ages, vegetables, oil,
water; it is dark, cold, warm; the temperature is
constant; lie the dead; there are worms, moles, ro-
dents, muskrats, gophers; there are catacombs; is
safe during a bombing; were the Partisans, early
Christians, Communists; it is interesting, mysterious,
valuable; lies my uncle; it is dirty; many feel
miserable; will be cold to lie; live the terrified mole
and the unseen worm; Hades.

57. *One can hardly see:*

What the future holds; what others think about
him; how he gets into trouble, his faults; what is
behind him; what is right; the end; interesting
things; in the dark, through the fog; when he is
tired, when his sight is failing; the sense in examinations like this; what good a family does; what is best
until it is too late.

58. *Wouldn't it be really funny if:*

We all got what we wanted; I won that new
Chrysler convertible, I became a millionaire; Joe
Stalin got knocked off, the Republicans won; there

were no more wars; I could quit drinking; I got well;
I passed this test; we won; people wore no clothes;
flying saucers were from Mars; people knew what
went on; everybody were alike; the doctor really
found out what my diagnosis is; animals could talk;
men started wearing dresses; houses could walk;
Chuck broke his neck; we were murdered; I could
get out of here; comics were funny; all the come-
dians on television got together some night and had
a program; grandmothers had wheels.

59. *The kind of animal I would like most to be:*

Dog, cocker spaniel, collie, puppy; cat, Siamese cat,
kitten; horse, stallion, race horse; human being, the
one I am, no animal; ape, monkey, marmoset; lion,
tiger, panther, leopard; bird, eagle, migratory bird;
deer, antelope; giraffe; elephant; mink; kangaroo;
whale; panda; rabbit; a cow because of her con-
tentment; a big steer; an anthropoid if not human; a
well-cared-for pet animal; the one that lives the
longest; with is a dog; sick is a snake.

60. *Nothing is harder to stop than:*

Fires, hurricanes, floods, lightning, a meteor; a fight,
a bullet; drinking, smoking, taking drugs, bad
habits; a train, a locomotive, a car going 90 mi. per
hr.; gossip, pests, a vicious tongue, a lie; arguing
with your wife; a drunk who doesn't give a damn;
a cold; enjoying yourself.

61. *The two most beautiful things I have ever seen:*

Are sunshine and trees; mountains; sunset and
water; the harbor in Rio and Kings Garden in Lon-
don; my father and mother, a baby's smile; were
both women; falling Jap planes and the U.S.A.; a

glass of beer and a dog; a $200 and a $500 check; I've never seen any.

62. *She couldn't bear to touch:*

The dead body, woman, mouse; him; his hand; his body; her husband; the hot stove; ice; the animal, dog, snake, frog, animal skin; anything slimy; the wet sponge; the knife; her painful jaw; the bloody casualty; her finger nails to a blackboard; anything belonging to someone else; upon certain subjects.

63. *A woman who has lost her virtue must:*

Regain it; do nothing, not worry about it; redeem herself; be unhappy; be happy, free, relieved; repent; conceal it; pay for it; remain virtueless, die in sin; face social opposition; not be condemned; not worry about it as another Kinsey report will back up her present beliefs; be interesting; start a new life in another town; redefine virtue for herself; not have wanted it much; have been in love; keep it a secret from all; not make a public issue of it; be like many others; must? huh? must she do anything in particular?; stay single; find it again; find an understanding man to marry.

64. *Failure may be expected when:*

One does not try, try hard enough; one is not prepared, not adequate for the task; you lack, lost, confidence; the obstacles are many and steep; you try too hard; you don't know enough; we believe it will occur; there is a will to fail; one is afraid to succeed; not feeling good; you're too frank; you can't get together; you try to do things without the help of God.

65. *An effeminate man may:*

Act like a woman; be a failure; be laughed at; be a
sissy, weak, a victim of circumstances; get in trouble, cause trouble; be peculiar, keep to himself; be
dangerous, deceive you; need help, have a mental
disease; be ostracized, be shunned; be autistic,
be attractive to some women; do well in some kinds
of work; make a good husband; get drunk; be disap-
pointed; be strong.

66. *It hurts when:*

You cut yourself, you burn your fingers; the dentist
drills; people are unkind; one is misunderstood; you
failed; you are punished; you have to admit you
have made a mistake; your best friend deceives you;
someone tells untrue things about you; you are hit
over the head; one sees people suffering and can't
help; someone you love doesn't love you; you have
done your best and no one appreciates it; people
continually ignore you.

67. *The deeper one goes:*

The more you understand; the less complex; the
more hopeful; the less confusing; the more he learns;
the hotter it gets; the more dangerous; the less he
knows; the more worms you find; the more apt to
find virtue; the darker it gets; the harder it gets;
the more morbid he becomes; the further he sinks;
the more trouble to get out of debt.

68. *Behind one's back:*

Unpleasant things are said, people talk, people
shouldn't talk; much happens; one doesn't know
what is going on; lies the past; the universe may dis-

appear; is the danger; they planned a surprise; one can always see by simply turning around; one cannot see the person's face; there is always someone if he's paranoid; space is largely unstructured; there is someone to knife you; came the car; there is his worst self.

69. *When the car skidded:*

The occupants, the driver, became frightened; the occupants were in danger; it crashed; the driver did the proper thing and regained control; the driver lost control; the driver tried to regain control; the car was overturned, went into a ditch, jumped the curb, ran into a pole; the driver woke up; everyone was afraid but me; it collided with another and caused a few casualties; he kept mumbling 'brake, brake'; we thought all would be over but we luckily escaped; it caused no damage; I steered automatically against the direction of the skid, though I knew better.

70. *A mother is more likely than a father to:*

Be understanding; be sympathetic, forgiving, lenient; influence her children; show affection; love daughter, son, more; spoil, be over protective to, pamper, her children; give in to her children; scold, be impatient, discipline; be at home with the children; be sensitive to children's needs; worry; defend, be loyal to her children; mistreat her children; obey her emotions; forgive my faults; be authoritative; help when you are ill; have a neurotic attachment to her son; worry about the sex problems of her daughter; need support and self-confidence; have headaches; remarry; cook dinner.

71. *The worst kind of criminal:*

Is a murderer; sex criminal; one who attacks children; one who steals from the poor, from the blind; intentional one; unintentional one; is the result of environmental forces; is hard to catch, is the one you can't catch; has some redeeming qualities; is one who denies guilt; is out for himself; is one that hurts another person; is me; needs understanding and consideration; is one who directs his actions to the promotion of world conflict for his own gain; is one that murders for no reason at all; is a hypocrite; is he who commits a crime against himself; is one who kidnaps; is a blackmailer; is an insane one; did not give his victim even a sporting chance.

72. *If one cannot own:*

A car he should ride the bus, doesn't need one, may be able to own a bicycle, can walk; a house he should, must, rent; an article he can borrow it; one learns to do without; something, one should not covet it; something, they feel despondent; what he wants, he must constantly strive for it; his necessities of life he should not feel insecure; up to his faults, he is a coward.

73. *Tests like this:*

Are helpful; are foolish; make one think; are interesting; show you up; are puzzling; are amusing; make one uncomfortable; make me wonder if I can trust you; may be informative; show how smart you are; are educational; are important; are probably necessary; are a pest; do not make sense; may mean something to somebody; are ridiculously inconclusive; are not, strictly speaking, "tests" at all.

After reading through the foregoing lists, one may have a feeling that he has sampled expressions of most of the important human hopes, fears, conflicts and rules of living. If so, these openings with their range of completions can provide a background against which a particular individual may be profitably set.

Chapter IV

INTERPRETATION: THE CASE OF ABNER

IT IS OFTEN DESIRABLE, as a first step, to read through the entire record without effort at interpretation. From this reading the examiner obtains a global impression which offers some protection against premature conclusions drawn from subsequent sentence by sentence analysis. Although it is never possible to retain a completely unbiased attitude after a few striking endings are encountered, one should try to defer general conclusions until the individual response is evaluated against the background of the total performance.

It is frequently useful to attend to groups of completions without reference to the sentence beginnings. The relationships between two responses to different openings are often closer and more obvious than the relationship of either completion to the beginning of its own sentence. Many of the personality characteristics revealed by a subject are more clearly delineated without than they are with reference to the openings.

After a global survey, and the identification of outstanding groups of responses, the possible significance of individual sentences should be explored. At this point, reference to illustrated endings in Chapter III will be useful. All variations of the response given should be considered, including direct opposites. Where a particular ending is altogether inconsistent with a larger picture delineated by other endings the discrepancy may indicate

(42)

areas of conflict and repression. It is sometimes difficult
to distinguish between inconsistencies within the personality itself and inconsistencies in the way in which it is
portrayed. Nevertheless, the effort must be made because
the distinction may be part of an appraisal of the relative
importance of specific conscious and unconscious attitudes.

It is usually helpful to record groups of related completions as premises with the logical inferences drawn by the
examiner from such groups. Not infrequently the same
logical inference, even though it is never explicit in any
sentence, will follow independently from two or more
groupings. Sometimes contradictory inferences are
drawn. When this happens it seems less likely that the
inconsistency represents a property of the portrayal than
of deeper conflict within the person.

As one proceeds through the sentences, vague structures
and outstanding properties begin to emerge. These clari-
fy themselves gradually with full use of the examiner's insight, empathy, and experience, until a personality picture in terms of basic conflicts, ways of handling conflict,
limitations and defects, as well as positive resources, has
developed.

Having outlined in broad terms some general suggestions on interpretation, we have chosen to provide a more
detailed discussion of interpretive procedure through the
analysis of a single record.

It is hard to recapture the exact reason for our selection
of Abner's record as an illustration of the technique of
analysis. It is neither dramatic nor wholly commonplace.
Yet it does provide examples of many of the kinds of problems in interpretation encountered in the use of sentence
completion.

Abner is a high school graduate, 22 years old, from a
lower middle-class family. His father is in a mental

hospital with a diagnosis of general paresis. For almost eight years Abner, an only child, has supported his mother. He was taken to a psychiatrist by his mother. He complained that there was something the matter with his mind and that he was losing his memory. The Wechsler-Bellevue showed an I. Q. of 120 (verbal 120, performance 118), with no evidence of memory impairment. His mother said that he did not act like other boys his age. He seemed never to want to go out and stayed home all the time.

In this record the sentence openings are in small capitals, the completions in bold face type. This will permit the reader to run quickly through the completions alone and obtain an impression of the general nature of the responses, apart from both the sentence openings and the authors' speculation and inference. After he has completed this he might then profitably read through the openings with the completions, still without reference to the interpretive comment.

In the running comments we attempt to illustrate our procedure in the analysis of a record. The items are considered in order, one at a time, until clusters of completions begin to emerge and the necessity for referring back and forward becomes clear·

It is not to be inferred that each analysis of a record necessarily involves the conscious reasoning outlined below. Obviously, the speed with which some conclusions may be reached precludes that possibility. However, it is certain that some conscious logical processes of this kind do occur in every interpretation. Many marginally conscious processes of the sort illustrated can be recognized, and it seems quite likely that many such trains of reasoning occur below a conscious level on the part of the interpreter.

Whether the narrative below is truly representative of
the actual reasoning, conscious and unconscious, of the
interpreters is debatable.

Every record contains some completions which are
conventional and seem to add little to the total picture.
In this record we have gone beyond the limits we normally
set in attempting to make use of every sentence, and have
made comments on some sentences to which we would
ordinarily pay little attention. However, we have at the
same time developed some sentences much less fully than
we might have.

In the version given this subject, certain openings noted
in the record had been deleted by our colleague who obtained the record. Sentence Number 46 had not yet been
added to the list at the time this subject was studied.

1. CHILDREN ARE USUALLY CERTAIN THAT **they are right.**

It did not occur to the subject to say that children
are usually certain that they are loved or that they can
have their own way. On the basis of our observation
that adults here often ascribe certainty to children in
areas of their own more important uncertainties, the
question raised at the outset is, "How right am I?" The
implication is that being right is important, and the
subject has some doubts about his judgment.

2. PEOPLE ARE PRAISED WHEN   **they do well.**

This is a common completion and suggests an acceptance of conventional values in reference to
achievement. Note the absence of indication of concern with competitive aspects of the situation: "they
succeed against odds," "they do exceptionally." Note
also the absence of reference to the feelings of others
when someone is praised: "they please others."

3. A LARGE CROWD   **is uncomfortable.**

This, unlike the two preceding ones, is a highly individual response. Its vagueness alone would make
it important. The crowd is not clearly defined as
existing outside of the person himself, and therefore
a question about the clarity of the subject's ego
boundaries is raised. In any case the affect is
unpleasant.

4. A PERSON IS MOST HELPLESS WHEN   **he is lost.**

The content of this response is distinctly unusual.
When this occurs one may consider the completion almost without reference to the opening. Even at this
early stage a picture begins to emerge; a lost soul, who
cannot clearly distinguish himself from the crowd, is
uncomfortable with it, is anxious to do well and hopes
against hope that he is right.

5. WHEN AN ANIMAL IS WILD   **he is feared.**

The animal, in sentence completion as in the Rorschach, often evokes reactions concerned with instinctive emotional aspects of the personality, and
responses to this item reflect something of a subject's
attitudes toward his more primitive drives and
impulses.

Sometimes a particularly interesting aspect of the
completion of this sentence is the choice of an active
or passive role: "it may attack people," or "it roams
the forest," versus, "it is feared," "it is to be avoided."

A second interesting aspect is the subject's interpretation, more often implicit than stated, of the term
"wild." Some subjects' picture of a wild animal is of
an animal which is not a domesticated one. For
others, wild means uncontrolled, or enraged. (Some

responses are ambiguous in this regard, for example, "it may bite.")

In this case, the passivity of role is outstanding, and this, as well as the anxiety aroused by a stimulus which relates to instinctive impulses, is consistent with the personality portrayed by the previous sentences.

6. THE HARDEST DECISIONS
                    to make involve things we love.

In hard decisions the difficulty may lie either in a conflict between specific alternatives or in the simple fact that a choice must be made. By the insertion of the awkward and unnecessary phrase, "to make," as well as by the ambiguous "things," this subject indicates that decisions per se represent so great an obstacle that he has difficulties in getting to the point of considering the actual issues involved.

So far there have been no indications of sensitivity to other people. The question whether "things" here include people must be left open. If people are implicitly included, the choice of an ambiguous term is important.

7. THE EASIEST WAY TO GET MONEY   **to work.**

The response "is to work for it" is the commonest of all responses to the opening, and has meaning only in terms of its consistency with the whole pattern. This subject's omission of "is" and "for it" emphasizes the importance for him of work itself in contrast to its goal. The responses "win it," "steal it," "marry it," would not be consistent with the passivity, anxiety, and conformity already exhibited.

8. TWENTY YEARS FROM NOW   **who knows what to expect.**

This opening offers the challenge of uncertainty,

and completions tend to reflect the extent of a subject's tolerance for it as well as to indicate something of the direction in which he turns in his efforts to reassure himself in the face of uncertainty.

Most completions involve speculation or hope or certainty about personal or social events: "the world will be very different," "there will be more inventions," "I will be 40," "I hope to be married." In this subject's completion, there is neither certainty nor speculation, nor even hope. There is only planlessness and a helpless acceptance of uncertainty. And, not only is he uncertain, but he seems to live in a world which everyone finds unpredictable. He projects his lack of assurance, and justifies the absence of plan in his life by asserting that other people are equally helpless.

9. PARENTS WOULD WORRY LESS IF   **I were their type.**

The shift to the first person singular and the explicit orientation of himself vis-a-vis his parents are certainly not required by the opening, constitute a rare form of response, and thus emphasize the importance of the parent-child relationship in his conceptual system. This completion, although making clear the element of hostility and rebelliousness, at the same time exposes the childish, petulant character of the protest. He does not say, for example, "Parents would worry less if / children were more like them."

In the sudden shift of reference there is a loss of detachment that is all the more marked because of the detached attitude of so many of his responses. It is as though he cannot maintain any objectivity when really personal problems are touched.

A struggle for a sense of personal identity is suggested by the use of "I" when rebellion against parents

is aroused and also in his use of the concept of "types."
He seems to try to understand his difficulties by ana-
lyzing them and trying to generalize about them. But
it is in his greatest efforts at objectivity that his greatest loss of detachment occurs.

10. WHEN FIRE STARTS   we must control ourselves.

The completion of this sentence usually seems to
reflect a subject's response to intense or sudden emotion. The commonest response is, "call the fire department," reflecting a tendency to call in relevant
authority when a situation is too difficult to handle
alone. In the completion next in frequency, "put it
out," the responsibility is taken by the subject. In
this instance the completion supports the earlier inference of helpless, ineffectual passivity and anxiety. He
is so busy controlling his own panic that he can neither
put the fire out nor even get help for that purpose.

Perhaps the panic aroused by the emotional challenge is what led to a reaction which appears at several
points in the record, a psychological gap between
stimulus and response. The chain of associations set
off by the opening may have been something like:
fire, danger, fear, panic, loss of control, necessity for
control. To jump from one end of the sequence to the
other omits too much, and thus is rather autistic.

This completion represents only one instance of an
emphasis on control which appears many times in the
record. It points up the importance of conscious control as a primary defense for this subject, and suggests
the presence of obsessive-compulsive features in the
personality.

The unusual use of the first person plural merits
some comment. Although rebellion against authority

seems to provide some basis for a sense of self (No. 9), the threat of emotional involvement destroys what tenuous sense of individuality he has, and sends him running for protection to identification with the group, as he did in another way in No. 8, but only to find it uncomfortable as he did in No. 2.

11. COMPARED WITH DOGS, CATS ARE
                              much more self centered.

The selection of this particular trait from the long list of possibilities implies that self-centeredness is at least important if not directly self-descriptive. Subjects are frequently inclined to ascribe to cats the distinctive properties which they associate with women.

12. FATHERS SHOULD LEARN THAT **age is not a handicap.**

Again, as in No. 10, there seems to be a logical gap between opening and completion. The associative sequence here is difficult, perhaps impossible, to reconstruct; the form of expression is highly individual. He may be trying to say something like: "Fathers should learn that just because their sons are grown and can take responsibility, there is no reason for the father to renounce responsibility." In the light of the history, this is one plausible interpretation. Or, he may be saying, "Fathers should learn that age is not a sufficient excuse for failure to fulfill the role of father." In any case, the statement is unclear and appears to be confused rather than abstract. The logical connection with the opening is weak, and again there is a suggestion of autism in his thinking.

Particular difficulty in the relationship with the father is suggested by the trouble he has expressing himself clearly in response to this opening. Perhaps even the suggestion implicit in the opening that fathers are imperfect and might be taught something, is too hard for him to handle, if the father has been harsh and punishing.

13. ONE'S CLOSEST FRIENDS CAN   **be irritating.**

The normal response to the concept of closeness of friendship involves strong feeling. One's closest friends may be "helpful" or "depended upon" in time of trouble. Or, they may "hurt one most" or "become one's worst enemies." Ordinarily they are not mildly pleasant or mildly disagreeable. This response really implies that the concept of close friendship has little meaning and there is little or no capacity for intimate personal relation.

14. IT IS EASY TO GET INTO TROUBLE WHEN   **you enjoy it.**

In the light of the picture of helplessness, unrelatedness, and discomfort that has so far emerged, this completion can be understood as an attempt to rationalize his own lack of enjoyment by pointing out that at least he stays out of trouble. He probably does not really live enough to get into trouble (see No. 15).

15. FEW CHILDREN FEAR   **life.**

A subject's principal fears are likely to be stated, sometimes with unexpected directness, sometimes more subtly, in his completion of this sentence. In these terms no response could be more hopeless or more depressed than this.

16. AT THE END OF THE ROAD   **there must be a turning.**

Rather than suggest that some constructive goal lies ahead, or even express negative feelings about the future, the subject demands the assurance of a second chance. This completion helps to confirm the impression of a helpless, planless person, who fears life itself with its implications of change which he can neither resist nor predict. The highly individual insistence that there *must* be a turning suggests a panicky conviction that he is already a failure.

17. HE DREW BACK FROM THE TOUCH OF   **coldness.**

Avoidance of cold may be based upon an appreciation of healthy, normal warmth. Also it may be based on an infantile need for protection. In this instance the latter explanation seems more appropriate. While cold objects (ice, steel, etc.) are frequently mentioned in completing this sentence, this subject's effort at abstract formulation is unusual. It seems to be another instance of the kind of detachment which has been noted earlier.

18. This item not included in version administered.

19. THE MOST PLEASANT DREAMS
       are those that combine fantasy and flattery.

It often happens that a single sentence provides a succinct statement of the essential character of the entire performance. Almost all the material before and after this sentence is given clarity by this intellectualized statement of the most compelling needs of this frustrated, ambitious, inadequate young man.

20. A DRUNKEN MAN   **can't compose anything.**

This completion has a bizarre, irrelevant, confused quality reminiscent of many completions by schizophrenics. The degree of control exhibited in preceding sentences appears to be lost at this point. It is possible that the direct self-revelation which occurred in the previous sentence is to some extent responsible

for the confusion in this one, a phenomenon which
has been observed in word association tests. However, the opening, "A drunken man," implying as it
does loss of conscious control, seems in this instance
sufficient basis for the confusion, since it is likely to
represent one of the subject's principal fears. One
wonders too about the ambiguous word "compose."
Does it mean to him creative accomplishment, or
orderly arrangement? Or does the confusion in expression arise from his confusion between the two
concepts?

21. No ONE CAN REPAIR THE DAMAGE CAUSED BY
others' non-thinking.

Whatever doubts there might have been heretofore
about the importance of conscious control and the
dangers in its loss are resolved by this completion. At
this point it is reasonable to look ahead to:

30. If people only knew how much / other people
    don't know.

40. The best of mothers may forget that / they
    don't understand.

41. There ought to be a law to / prevent misunder-
    standings.

50. There would be more divorces if / there were
    less education.

53. One's best friend may be irritating when /
    they disagree.

Note that it is not just thoughtlessness but *others'*
non-thinking that causes irreparable damage. It is
out of such conceptual matrices as these that paranoid
systems ordinarily develop. If he can acquire suffi-

cient knowledge, and thereby power, he can achieve superiority without the emotional involvement with others which he resists so strongly.

22. THE NICEST THING ABOUT BEING A CHILD
is freedom from responsibility.

This completion and No. 29, "Children are most annoying when / they become irresponsible," constitute a clear contradiction in his conceptual system; a contradiction which remains unreconciled throughout the record. For him the most annoying property of children is their nicest property. He wants freedom from responsibility and at the same time recognizes the impropriety of satisfying that desire.

23. THERE IS HARDLY ANY **need for worry.**

There is hardly any opening in the series with the possible exception of "Wouldn't it be really funny if" which is so deceptively unstructured as this one. One would expect it to be easy to give a straightforward factual statement about an area of scarcity. However, with surprising frequency the subject selects this opening as an occasion for making a pronouncement on an issue which either is or he hopes is controversial. With Abner's need for certainty and lack of basis for it one can understand his hope that worry is unnecessary.

24. TO BE WITHOUT SHAME **is to be without...**

At least he started to respond. A life in which shame and guilt are not the core might well be inconceivable to him even though he has just observed that "There is hardly any / need for worry."

25. WORSE THAN BEING LONELY IS **being longed for.**
This is another queer autistic response in which it is

difficult to insert a logical chain between opening and completion. He may be saying, "The worst thing that could happen to me would be the assumption of responsibility. Nothing would impose more responsibility on me than another person's emotional dependence. Therefore one of the worst things that can happen, worse even than loneliness, is another's longing for me." Compare Nos. 3, 4, 6, 11, 13, 17, 19, and 21.

26. WHEN A PERSON IS ILL   **life is harder.**

This is an isolated, passive, dull, depressed response. The use of the comparative reemphasizes earlier assertions that life at best is hard. This is not the kind of response given by a person who would be likely to use somatic disorder as an escape from difficulty.

27. A MAN CAN STOP BEATING HIS WIFE ONLY IF

(no response).

This is the only opening for which no completion was attempted. A facetious answer, sometimes utilized to avoid frank acceptance of aggression, is not possible for Abner, who seems incapable of a light touch.

28. THE BEST THING ABOUT OLD AGE   **is relaxation.**

If this sentence is taken in conjunction with No. 22, "The nicest thing about being a child / is freedom from responsibility," and both are oriented to his own aversion to responsibility, he seems to be asserting that any other time is better than the present. This is consistent with the depressed tone of most of the responses.

29. CHILDREN ARE MOST ANNOYING WHEN
they become irresponsible.
See No. 22. He does not see how absurd it is to
assume that a child should be responsible. Perhaps
he has never experienced freedom from the demand
for responsibility—never has had the opportunity
really to be a child.

30. IF PEOPLE ONLY KNEW HOW MUCH
other people don't know.
See No. 21.

31. THE MAIN DIFFERENCE BETWEEN A WILD AND A TAME
ANIMAL IS
their disposition.
Empty, high-sounding generalizations, apparent abstractions which have only a spurious logic are the
rule when Abner is confronted with feeling, impulse,
aggression, or anything really alive.

32. FEW THINGS ARE LESS ATTRACTIVE THAN
money.
The examiner, on the basis of other evidence, con-
siders that the opening was read by the subject as
written—"less" attractive. Often, the opening is an-
swered as if it had been read "more" attractive. Thus,
the subject alleges his interest in the higher things of
life only. Inasmuch as the base realities in terms of
responsibility for food, clothing and shelter are actually very important to him, his exclusive attention to
higher values adds weight to the judgment of a paranoid characteristic in his thinking.

33. THE WORST THING ABOUT BEING SICK
enclosed, being enclosed.
The element of confinement is not unusual in this
sentence; Abner's choice of words, however, is idio-

syncratic and therefore important. "Enclosed" may be more truly representative of his psychological situation than "confined." Note that being enclosed is here related to sickness which is one of the things which make life harder.

34. IT IS OFTEN HARD TO SLEEP WHEN **you're nervous.**

Again an expression of the anxiety and tension which pervade the record. See especially Nos. 23 and 28.

35. PEOPLE SHOULDN'T **speak ill.**

The general sense of this completion is usual enough—people shouldn't gossip, say harsh things about others, etc. However, the archaic language justifies some emphasis on its significance. Taken in context with the cluster noted in No. 21, it adds conviction to the suspicion of paranoid thinking. He feels that the effectiveness of his conscious control is threatened not only by others' non-thinking but by their hostility.

36. TO BE A GOOD LIAR ONE MUST **practice.**

This is a dull, unimaginative response which fails to differentiate between lying and any other skill, playing the piano, for instance.

37. This item not included in version administered.

38. PEOPLE REFRAIN FROM MURDER ONLY BECAUSE **of the psychological consequences.**

This response is another evasive generalization in which he avoids facing clear aggression. The magic of knowledge and long words helps to coin a phrase which takes care of the situation without his committing himself. Neither sanity, good will, civilizing forces on the one hand, nor purely selfish considerations such as fear, penalties, and the like are perceived by him as adequate deterrents.

39.   TOO MUCH DISTANCE LIES BETWEEN   **friends.**

This completion is a surprisingly direct statement of his isolation and lack of capacity for close relations with people.

40.   THE BEST OF MOTHERS MAY FORGET THAT

                           they don't understand.

With the feeling he has of distance from his parents (No. 9), the sense of childhood deprivation (No. 29), and the emphasis on intellectual understanding (No. 21 cluster), this completion scarcely calls for further comment in terms of the mother-child relationship.

It may, however, be profitable to examine more closely the form of the sentence. He says that the best of mothers may forget that they don't understand. Does he mean to imply that the best of mothers at one time or another have been aware that they don't understand? Such a warm and sophisticated understanding of mothers is certainly out of character for Abner. Does he then mean perhaps that everyone knows that mothers don't understand, and he uses the term "forget" as it is often used colloquially to indicate that which has never been apprehended as, "You forget that he is 'this,' or 'that,'" when indeed you have never known it and may even consider it to be untrue. This seems to be closer to Abner's pattern. If so he has done what schizophrenics often do in sentence completion—make an assertion which is important to him but has minimal relevance to the opening.

41. THERE OUGHT TO BE A LAW TO
                    prevent misunderstanding.

(See No. 21) This bizarre idea that one might invoke law to achieve that which can so clearly be achieved only through interpersonal relations now leaves no doubt as to the disorganization of thinking.

42. SPIDERS ARE   **insects.**

In a group of dull, defeated, hopeless old men this was by far the commonest response. In a group of young active men far more comparable to this subject in social background, and occupational level, the response was given by only a small minority. Active, descriptive phrases were the rule.

43. WHEN A CRIMINAL LEAVES THE PRISON HE
                    wonders when he will be back.

In No. 33, he says, "The worst thing about being sick / enclosed, being enclosed." The wish for freedom and the fear of its consequences are in direct conflict. He would like to be independent and successful, but this would mean taking responsibility, and he feels too helpless and hopeless to dare to act without externally imposed restraint. A satisfactory solution might lie in the construction of such barriers as will completely isolate him from outside intrusions and still permit absolute freedom of movement within his own fantasy.

44. COMPARED WITH SISTERS, BROTHERS ARE
                    of the same family.

Sisters versus brothers is a differentiation which most people can make easily. At least there is usually little effort to dodge the issue of unlikeness. His uncertainty about sexual differentiation, subtly implied in many sentences heretofore, is now brought out into the open. Where comparisons are demanded, for example in conventional intelligence tests, differences are often resorted to where similarities are difficult. In this instance differences, the primitive and easy differentiation, are not cited. They are of the *same* family.

45. THE FINGER POINTED   **at him.**

Here is another relatively common response, one which in itself would not justify a judgment about paranoid trends but now in this case supports such an inference.

46. This item not included in version administered.

47. TO AVOID A FIGHT ONE MUST   **use tact.**

For Abner to complete in so simple and direct a fashion a sentence involving aggression seems strange. The explanation may be that this is one of the few instances in which a conventional response coincides with Abner's way of reacting.

48. This item not included in version administered.

49. CLOSER AND CLOSER THERE COMES   **conflict.**

In these days the conflict about which subjects show concern is more often international than personal. In this case we conclude that the conflict which he fears is within himself and represents a condition for which Abner has a low tolerance.

50. THERE WOULD BE MORE DIVORCES IF
                          there were less education.

(See No. 21)

51. A DRUNKEN WOMAN   **exhibits weakness.**

He can remain coherent when discussing weakness

of conscious control in women, who are permitted by custom to exhibit it, in contrast to his confusion in response to a drunken man. This contrast may be a verbal assertion of his masculinity about which he is uncertain.

52. WHEN A PERSON IS WOUNDED **he feels pain.**

Here again he is alone, passive and unaided, identifying with the victim rather than with the onlooker or helper. In this sentence, as in so many, the reference is static and without orientation to the future.

53. ONE'S BEST FRIEND MAY BE IRRITATING WHEN

they disagree.

(See No 21.) In this sentence the reference to disagreement, with the intellectual emphasis already noted, ignores the universally recognized properties of friendship. He has no real friends. This is a highly egocentric response. It suggests an inability to brook opposition, to recognize another's point of view. No wonder he feels so rejected. His concept of social relationship permits no individual expression.

54. This item not included in version administered.

55. A WEAK PERSON DOES NOT OFTEN **succeed.**

This seems to be a straightforward self-descriptive statement with a depressive tone.

56. DOWN UNDERGROUND **are the mysteries of life—I was going to say life, but that's not it.**

In this sentence Abner really seems to go to pieces. It is confused and autistic, as well as depressed. The magic of the phrase "mysteries of life" fails to satisfy even his low requirements for coherent logical thought.

57. ONE CAN HARDLY SEE   everything.

This completion again brings in the theme of Abner's need to encompass within his consciousness all that goes on around him. This sentence might reasonably be further construed as an assertion that there is nothing which he can really see. See No. 4, "A person is most helpless when / he is lost."

58. WOULDN'T IT BE REALLY FUNNY IF
                    we discovered that everything wasn't real.

Completions for this sentence are often most unfunny. They may represent strong hopes which one almost despairs of realizing or strong fears which one hesitates to admit. In this case it may well be both.

59. THE KIND OF ANIMAL I WOULD LIKE MOST TO BE
                              is some clean animal.

Many people who find themselves unable to identify with an animal insist on their identity only with humans. He neither identifies with a particular animal nor insists on his humanness but gives a noncommital response which illustrates the close association between his anxiety and feelings of guilt and his animal impulses. One would not be surprised if obsessive ideas about cleanliness were present. Note, too, the phobic implications of Nos. 3 and 33.

60. NOTHING IS HARDER TO STOP THAN   motion.

Throughout the record there have appeared abstractions of doubtful logical validity. This is one of the most clearly spurious of his abstractions. One may ask, "What in the world can be stopped except motion?" It is as though he says "Nothing is harder to stop than that which has been started," or conversely, "Whatever has started cannot be stopped." This strengthens the impression that he feels a complete lack of control and surrender to compulsion.

61. THE TWO MOST BEAUTIFUL THINGS I HAVE EVER SEEN
                                    were symmetrical.

In many respects he resembles the Rorschach subject who instead of saying that a card looks like this or that says, "There is a line down the center which holds the two sides together." The necessity for maintenance of rigid form and order extends even to the determination of Abner's esthetic values.

62. SHE COULDN'T BEAR TO TOUCH   **the wound.**

Considering this sentence as the beginning of a sequence, follow with "When a person is wounded / he feels pain, It hurts when / you realize you've been wrong, Children are usually certain that / they are right, and so we go full circle to, The best of mothers may forget that / they don't understand, and the solution, There ought to be a law to /prevent misunderstandings, but, since this in reality is impossible, Wouldn't it be really funny if / we discovered that everything wasn't real, and There is hardly any / need for worry."

63. A WOMAN WHO HAS LOST HER VIRTUE MUST   **repent.**

This seems to be such a simple, easy, conventional solution that we would expect it to appear frequently. It doesn't. In this case it may reflect his verbal efforts to extricate himself from difficulty and his conventional posture in the face of guilt.

64. FAILURE MAY BE EXPECTED WHEN
                          not enough initiative is used.

With No. 55, A weak person does not often / succeed, he says in effect that weakness lies in the lack of initiative, in not getting started. But since he dare not get started because his control is inadequate and he will be unable to stop (see No. 60) he is trapped and doomed to failure, unless of course "we discovered that everything wasn't real."

65. This item not included in version administered.

66. IT HURTS WHEN   **you realize you've been wrong.**

Here again the "right-wrong" axis and the egocentricity which puts the source of pain within the person rather than in relation with others. He emphasizes his failure to live up to his intellectual standards, unrealistic as they are.

67. THE DEEPER ONE GOES   **the more involved he becomes.**

In No. 56, Abner said that "Down underground / are the mysteries of life," rather than life. Evidently he is becoming more deeply involved in its mysteries and less in life itself. This is not surprising considering his fear of life (No. 15).

68. BEHIND ONE'S BACK   **the world revolves.**

In this completion, which is analogous to an abstract *m* Rorschach response, there is intense, immobile isolation in the midst of uncontrollable forces, which strengthens the inferences of schizophrenic development.

69. WHEN THE CAR SKIDDED   **there was a sounding crash.**

The crash or accident is not unusual in this sentence. In most crashes, however, the auditory component is relatively unimportant to the participant as compared with the bystander. Thus we have Abner, certain of catastrophe, but maintaining detachment as usual.

70. A MOTHER IS MORE LIKELY THAN A FATHER TO
understand her daughter.

It is as though he could take care of two problems
in this one completion. He can, in effect, support his
denial of maternal understanding and at the same time
can give expression to the feeling that if he were a girl
he might get the understanding which he wants. If
this interpretation is correct, he would in this respect
be like many other paranoid schizophrenics. This
sentence should serve as a warning against a too direct
and literal interpretation of completions. Even if
Abner had a sister, jealousy should not be imputed to
him without a sophisticated psychological interpretation of its meaning.

71. THE WORST KIND OF CRIMINAL,
is the one who doesn't care.

This seems to be a statement of Abner's intense
sense of guilt about his attitude toward responsibility.
He cannot really mean that if one cared about some
particular thing or some particular person he would
therefore be less of a criminal. He probably is saying
that caring itself is the difference between the criminal and noncriminal. The assumption of responsibility
itself is important.

72. IF ONE CANNOT OWN
one must borrow.

Compare No. 14, "It is easy to get into trouble
when / you enjoy it," and No. 36, "To be a good liar
one must / practice."

This cluster might raise a question of a psychopathic
component. However, the total picture offers no support for the inference that such a pattern is a major
factor in the maladjustment. It is worth noting that

whatever of this picture does occur is quite consistent with the immaturity and rejection of responsibility which are unquestionably major factors in his schizophrenic pattern.

73. This item not included in version administered.

Abner now emerges as a member of a diagnostic group which seems to be increasing in size even though its definitive boundaries are still unclear to psychiatrists and psychologists who are brought face to face with its members in the course of their professional work. This group, when it is given a name, is often called the "ambulatory schizophrenic." With the use of newer and more penetrating diagnostic instruments and their application to people who would heretofore never have been examined, we begin to find disorganization in thinking, inability to relate emotionally to others, paranoid ideas, a growing sense of loss of control and feeling of unreality, and a tendency to withdraw into compensatory fantasy. These properties are not always, indeed not often, associated necessarily with the dramatic events which in the past have been cited as 'evidence' of schizophrenia. The person does go to work, he does go to the barber, he does not allege that he is Napoleon or that he is being persecuted by the Government, his bizarre gestures attract little attention, but he operates in daily affairs with minimum effectiveness. The crucial difference between this "ambulatory schizophrenic" and his counterpart who clearly requires institutional care, is that the former maintains successfully certain defenses which are insufficient to protect the latter. These defenses themselves are perceptible in the sentence completion. For Abner they include a great and effective stress on *conscious control*. They include too a rigid adjustment which at best looks like an escape into work, a search for power through knowledge, and an over-reliance on abstract thinking in lieu of feeling in interpersonal relations. At worst these manifestations are considered to be obsessive compulsive or phobic symptoms.

It is as though Abner had adult responsibility thrust upon him too early, without the opportunity to obtain the childhood support and satisfactions which might have given him the strength to assume responsibility as a mature individual. He is deeply afraid of life and, confronted by the growing recognition that by his own standards he is a failure, he seems to be seeking security by withdrawing from others into an unreal if rather impoverished fantasy life.

If life does not demand of him any important decisions or any real independence, it is possible that he can maintain his brittle, unhappy surface adaptation indefinitely.

Abner's Rorschach record, which follows, was not available to the writers until after the foregoing interpretations had been completed. This record is appended as an illustration of the clear consistency which may be found when sentence completion and Rorschach materials are compared.

I.   **Right side up?**
30″ ∨ 1.   **Reminds me of a pumpkin on a Hallowe'en.**
    ∧ 2.   **This may look like a bat laid out on display or something.**
60″
Inquiry

Pumpkin face — except for the fact that it is not completely round it reminds me of it. There are eyes and the exaggeration of a nose and the bottom where the mouth should be without any closure and this should be the stem of the pumpkin. (The upper edge of the mouth is at the bottom rim of the white space.)

Bat — That is, held this way. (What gives you the impression?) It is stretched out first of all, and it's black and it appears to have a tail which is part bone.

All of these are symmetrical, all suggest one complete thing or two things opposed to each other of similar characteristics.

II. 7″ ∧ 1.   Looks like two clowns dancing (laughs).
What else could it look like? That's all I could
see out of it.

    34″

Inquiry

Red hoods with cutouts for the eyes and mouth. Their two hands are together. They had draped costumes. They look a little morbid — all one color. They are dancing so fast that sparks are flying out of the junction of their feet.

III. 7″ ∧ 1.   Looks like two little chicks pulling on something, I don't know what.
I don't know what the red is there.

    23″

Inquiry

Chicks — there are two chicks tugging on something that looks like a bone. Their heads are shaped like chicks with a bill. The bodies are not complete in the roundness and oval form. Their feet stick out like the bony affairs that they have, and the part in the middle looks like the breastbone of some animal. (Additional) ∨ This might signify ballet dancers with their feet kicking up, but their feet do not look like it.

(Additional) ∧ This reminds me of palm trees here (outer red).

IV. 8″ ∧ 1.   Looks like a giant bear, as if you had an ant-side view of him—his big feet and big tail.

    35″

Inquiry

This is the giant bear with the enormous feet. I am looking up from the ground and see the large tail in the back. It is fuzzy, enough to have the texture of a bear's hide. The rest is just the general shape.

V. 15″ ⌄ 1.   Looks like a butterfly.

    ⌃ **2.   This way it looks like two people standing on a rock and a big wave coming to envelop them — two people with a high hairdress.**

  49″

Inquiry

Butterfly — This is the butterfly, especially with the antenna affair and the general contour of the wings. It reminds me of some type of moth or insect and it has the general dimensions and localization of the butterfly.

Two people — there is a whole black wave coming up and two people are standing on the rock. (Headdress?) They have a high coiffure. (What kind of people?) One looks like a man and one looks like a woman.

VI.   55″ ⌃ 1.   Only thing I can see it looks like is aerial photography of a canal and parts of the surrounding territory.

  72″

Inquiry

This is an aerial view of a river or a railroad track. The depth of perception into shading as if you are looking at it from a plane.

(Additional) ⌃ This distraction up here looks like it could be some kind of an insect too with the wings.

(Additional) ⌃ This way looks like two caterpillars or worm-like insects meeting at the junction point of a cutaway tunnel into the earth.

VII.   33″ ⌃ 1.   Looks like two Easter bunnies laughing. I am not very imaginative.

  47″

Inquiry

These are two Easter bunnies. They are round and soft and their facial features are laughing. The lower part is missing but you are oblivious to it. I can't get anything out of that.

VIII. 15″ ∧ 1.   It doesn't look right that way. (Turns) (Turns again). Looks like some type of four-footed animal holding on to the roots of a tree and something is dripping down from the tree into a crevasse or a canyon.

45″

Inquiry

These are the two four-footed animals on either side, muskrats or wolves, climbing up a tree suspended in the air.   There is substance or sap dripping down the center of the tree and it hits here and changes color.   (From what position is it seen?) As if I were standing at the end of a canyon and looking down at it.   There is just the barest suggestion here that looks like a waterfall and this looks like an embankment.   It is stretching it, but it might be it.

IX. 20″ ∨ 1.   Looks like four elephants on top looking down into a skull surrounded on either side with dark smoke and at the bottom of that there are two birds with a large head and two claws.

60″

Inquiry

Four elephants at the top looking down.   Their eyes are high up and there is a trunk and tusk there.   The four are in line because they are so close together.   In the middle it looks like the skull of a mammal or a steer.   On the side is the egg-shaped head of a bird with its claws and tail portion here. There is dark smoke billowing from the top of the skull, possibly it suggests deterioration which makes it more ominous. The openings here, long slits, accentuate the shape and there is a difference in shading—the dark part looks like the shadow inside of the skull.   It suggests a skull because it's light like bone color.

X.   6″ ∧ 1.   The top looks like two types of toad animals.
 2.   And the bottom looks like two caterpillars staring a rabbit in the eye.
 3.   The yellow spots on either side look like dogs.
 4.   The two red spots look like the face of a gorilla.

> That's about all I can squeeze out of that. All
> I can get is animals out of them.

75"

Inquiry

Toad — it has large eyes and a squeezed body and short legs.
Caterpillars — they are green and have short legs sticking out
at the bottom. The legs should be all along but it is only at
the bottom and you can see their heads with eyes. The rabbit
has little ears sticking up and white accents for the little nose.
The eyes of the caterpillar are at the place for the rabbit's eyes.
Dogs — the yellow blots look like expensive Pekingese dogs
posing. They have shiny fur and a long nose.
Gorillas — the red part looks like two gorillas staring at each
other. Something is hanging down from their mouths but I
don't know what.

Like best:

No. III — because it is simple, easily comprehended, and gives
the essence of what it is supposed to represent. The colors are
not too harsh and it doesn't clash in arrangement. It looks
logical with nothing haphazard about it.

Like least:

No. VII — because it doesn't make any sense. There is no con-
tinuity here. It is balanced but not satisfying.

Testing the limits:

Butterfly? — (Could find none in color card. Does not accept
III because "doesn't have antenna or any body structure there."
Accepts the same portion as a hairbow.)

Smoke and fire? — (picks Cards IX) "because the red down
here is the closest to fire and smoke. Something is burning
giving off all kinds of fumes like rotten wood. Darker and
lighter fumes all mixed together."

Blood? — (picks Card VIII) "because it has the appearance of
a body laid open and the skin pulled back with the different
showing, and the blood near the surface internally. The blue
and red and in-between shades might remind you of venous
or arterial blood."

Chapter V

ILLUSTRATIVE RECORDS

THE RECORDS in this chapter are included to illustrate the variety of useful diagnostic material which may be obtained from widely differing subjects and under varied conditions. The comments which preface and follow the records are not intended as illustrative of the reports which the authors would write on these records in a clinical setting. They are meant to point out highlights and to provide leads to the reader in his exploration of the records.

1. BENJAMIN

The question often arises, "How susceptible are these sentences to completions in which the respondent creates an impression in accordance with his own immediate purposes, thus concealing the more important facets of his personality?" There is no final answer now to this question, and we concede its fairness. It has seemed to us, however, that usually an effort to create a façade, or to cover up, results only in a more transparent production. It is as if the defenses of the unconscious are a far more effective screen against both one's own and another's interpretations than are the conscious constructs from the well developed cerebrum.

One trouble with an experimental attack on the problem is that one is never quite sure about how seriously the respondent would take instructions to reply facetiously if they were so given. In the case of Benjamin, no instructions were given beyond those on the printed text, "Complete each sentence in whatever way you wish. If you have trouble thinking of a completion to any sentence, put a circle around the number, and return to the sentence when you have finished the rest." He spontaneously elected to do as he did and prefaced his completions as follows:

"Being quite in the dark concerning the purpose of this test and the nature of the conclusions to be drawn from my performance, I am purposely giving two completions to each sentence, one intended to be serious and one frivolous. The serious completions are always given first, the frivolous always second."

Benjamin is a man in his early sixties. He is a good friend of one of the authors. Sentences 10, 23, and 58 have been slightly altered to conceal his identity. He has lived an exciting and rich life, but he depreciates his achievements and abilities, making a public spectacle of his attention to the inconsequential. He is capable of inestimable warmth and depth of feeling. He has a brilliant intellect, with professional psychological insights, of which he is probably very proud, but which he would be the first to deny, if pushed into serious argument. He is the good father of two children by his first wife, from whom he is divorced, and a satisfactory husband of his second wife, with whom he has lived for more than 20 years.

It will be abundantly clear to the reader, as it was to Benjamin himself before he completed the task, that the seriousness or frivolousness of a subject's intent is not necessarily reflected in the response. Benjamin's comment on the procedure as a whole appears on the flyleaf.

1. *Children are usually certain that*

    Other children are more interesting than grownups.

    Circuses rate above Sunday school in entertainment.

2. *People are praised when*

    Others regard them as praiseworthy.

    They do good.

3. *A large crowd*

    Is not easily taken in your stride.

    Can easily consist of three persons — two lovers and a chaperone.

4. *A person is most helpless when*

    He can help neither himself nor others.

    He is a drug addict and has no possible access to his drug.

5. *When an animal is wild*

    It usually dies an accidental death.

    It is merely somewhat more of a nuisance than when it is tame.

6. *The hardest decisions*

    Are made when one's self-interest is opposed to the interests of others or of the whole.

    Are made by checker players who have only a choice of bad moves.

7. *The easiest way to get money*

    Is to be born rich.

    Is to be mistress of a king.

8. *Twenty years from now*

    Conveniences and inventions little dreamed of now will be commonplace in every museum.

    The writer, if alive, will be twenty years older.

9. *Parents would worry less if*

    They were happily married.

    If they had less to worry about.

10. *When fire starts*

    In (Name of city), call (Tel. No.)

    In a frying pan, put salt, NOT water on it.

11. *Compared with dogs, cats are*

Usually more liked by women than by men. Better catchers of birds and mice.

12. *Fathers should learn that*

Though they may think of themselves as their children's best friend, the children require proof of this beyond mere admonition and advice. Sons grow up.

13. *One's closest friends can be*

One's worst interpreter. Be one's most negligent correspondents.

14. *It is easy to get into trouble when*

You are hungry and the larder is bare. Your opponent at poker is a better bluffer than you are.

15. *Few children fear*

Loving parents. Their second Teddy Bear.

16. *At the end of the road*

Die as gracefully as possible. Hire a construction company to extend it to the next highway.

17. *He drew back from the touch of*

Her clammy hand. The warmth of her lips against his, thus giving his rival a clear advantage.

18. *The white girl who married the colored man*

Did so because—and why not? she loved him and he loved her. Did so because his child was already in her belly and she hated shotguns.

19. *The most pleasant dreams*

Are the dreams of youth. Are those your wife cannot remember next morning.

20. *A drunken man*

Is, sir, by my soul, a man intoxicated — not, begging pardon, with love, but with alcohol.

Fouleth his sheets.

21. *No one can repair the damage caused by*

Religious wars and fanaticisms.

Irresponsible character assassins who lie, libel and slander whilst smirking behind Congressional immunity.

22. *The nicest thing about being a child*

Is that you are not an adult.

Is that, if you live long enough, you will cease to be one.

23. *There is hardly any*

Lobster stew better than (examiner's).

Way to complete a sentence which begins "There is hardly any—"

24. *To be without shame*

Is to be incapable of feeling shame.

For any act of your life is tantamount to having performed no acts in the course of your life.

25. *Worse than being lonely is*

To be unloved.

To be under the necessity of attending all the cocktail parties to which you are invited.

26. *When a person is ill*

He will either get better, get worse, or remain the same.

It is high time for him to make a will—unless he prefers to die intestate.

27. *A man can stop beating his wife only if*

He has already beaten her. She reforms.

28. *The best thing about old age*

Is that it augurs the approach of death.

Is Old Age Security Insurance.

29. *Children are most annoying when*

They reach the "why? The contraceptive failed and no
why, why?" age. abortionist could be found.

30. *If people only knew how much*

Money they spend in rent Sorry: no space.
over 20 yrs., they would
start buying their own
homes with their baptis-
mal presents.

31. *The main difference between a wild and a tame animal is*

Indistinct and unimpor- The difference between Samuel
tant, especially in the Johnson and Lord Chesterfield
councils of the U. N. at table.

32. *Few things are less attractive than*

U. S. Route No. 1 be- The hind end of a horse with tail
tween New York and raised, relieving itself, when you
Washington. are taking your girl friend out for
your 1st drive.

33. *The worst thing about being sick*

Is the personal discom- Is the knowledge that your doc-
fort suffered by the pa- tors are liars first and doctors af-
tient. terward.

34. *It is often hard to sleep when*

Your wife has been away You are not sleepy.
for a week and the sheets
seem unduly cold.

35. *People shouldn't*

Believe all they read in Read only newspapers presenting
the newspapers. die-hard GOP points of view.

36. *To be a good liar one must*

Be a competent actor. Have a plausible story.

37. *A masculine woman should*

Be recognizable at sight Be capable, when necessary, of
by the experienced and being a female man.
discriminating.

38. People refrain from murder only because

The desire or impulse to murder is successfully off-set by weightier behavior determinants.	There's always a policeman around at the propitious time.

39. Too much distance lies between

Earth and moon for man yet to feel confident of ever making the round trip.	The two events to justify your comparison.

40. The best of mothers may forget that

There has never been a perfect child or a perfect mother.	Their husbands are not always the best of fathers.

41. There ought to be a law to

Define more clearly the powers of the President.	Permit occasional lapses from so-called sexual morality.

42. Spiders are

Poor bedfellows.	The joy of only perverted entomologists.

43. When a criminal leaves the prison he

Either hopes to go straight or to avoid be-'ing caught thereafter.	Is seldom heard to mutter: "This served me right and made a better man of me."

44. Compared with sisters brothers are

More loyal and affectionate.	Less considerate of parents.

45. The finger pointed

Directly at me.	At the author of the test, whose face reddened with embarrassment.

46. Children are least annoying when

Loved.	Asleep.

47. *To avoid a fight one must*

Often show the white feather.

Have demonstrated his ability to lick all comers.

48. *A naked man*

Is usually less impressive than when fully clothed.

Is fit to lie with a woman.

49. *Closer and closer there comes*

The season of bock beer.

The last of these sentences to be completed.

50. *There would be more divorces if*

Both religious and legal codes were redrafted by persons already divorced.

People married younger.

51. *A drunken woman*

Is more easily raped than a sober one.

Is a woman with money to spend if she pays for her own liquor.

52. *When a person is wounded*

In battle, he is everybody's hero.

In a saloon brawl, he is nobody's hero.

53. *One's best friend may be irritating when*

He praises you in public.

He scratches you with a stiff brush.

54. *A woman's body*

Differs in important ways from a man's.

Is a rag, a bone and a hank of hair.

55. *A weak person does not often*

Overcome a strong one.

Put up a fight until every retreat has been cut off.

56. *Down underground*

Lie the mistakes of the doctors, whereas the mistakes of lawyers live to mock them.

Are the favored working places for miners, moles and archeologists.

57. *One can hardly see*

What is exactly at the horizon.

The purpose of a silly exercise like the Miale-Holsopple Sentence Completion.

58. *Wouldn't it be really funny if*

Oliver Wendell Holmes had dared to write as funny as he can?

(Examiner) should win our pending checker game.

59. *The kind of animal I would like most to be*

Is one not yet produced by the process of evolution.

Is one of the extinct animals.

60. *Nothing is harder to stop than*

An irresistible force.

The groundswell for General Eisenhower.

61. *The two most beautiful things I have ever seen*

Are the Aurora Borealis and a violet.

A checkbook showing a sizeable balance and an empty folder labelled "Unpaid Bills."

62. *She couldn't bear to touch*

The memories of the past, lest they become hobgoblins of the present.

A single key, lest he discover that she was not a piano player.

63. *A woman who has lost her virtue must*

Have been either attractive or mercenary.

Pay heavily in the confessional.

64. *Failure may be expected when*

Even Eddie Arcaro rides a 50-to-1 shot.

The next assault is made on Mt. Everest.

65. *An effeminate man may*

And probably will, marry a masculine woman.

Be Mars himself behind the footlights.

66. *It hurts when*

One of Joe Louis's left hooks lands.

Birthdays are forgotten.

67. *The deeper one goes*

Into contemporary psy-   The lower one gets.
chology, the less sure one
is that it has a sound
scientific basis.

68. *Behind one's back*

Slanderers ply their   Rips in coat seams cause titters
tongues.   among one's followers.

69. *When the car skidded*

The driver, with rare self-   It merely backed up to the near-
possession, let go of the   est White Tower.
wheel, thus causing the
death of only his wife and
children, whereas he him-
self was unhurt.

70. *A mother is more likely than a father to*

Feel the pangs of child-   Be the first to see the new-born
birth.   babe.

71. *The worst kind of criminal*

May get the lightest sen-   May rise to rulership in a despo-
tence.   tism.

72. *If one cannot own*

All that he covets, let him   A harem, let him be content with
be content with what he   selected mistresses.
can get by fair means.

73. *Tests like this*

Are, on the part of the   Words fail.
testers, sadistic; on the
part of the tested, mas-
ochistic; and on the part of
all others, merely fruitless,
or deserving and receiving
satire.

2. CHARLES

Charles in 44 years old. He finished high school at the age of 17, and at 19 entered military service. After a year he developed a mental disorder originally diagnosed as a manic-depressive psychosis, manic type. There followed an unstable adjustment as a nomad laborer, 13 periods of hospitalization, excessive use of alcohol and delirium tremens.

Prior to a lobotomy operation his behavior pattern was one of periodic stereotyped, condescending behavior, interspersed with short episodes of lucidity and adjustment followed by extreme confusion, hyperactivity and auditory hallucinations.

Following surgery he showed marked change. He appeared less rigid, manneristic, and incoherent. His anxiety symptoms were gone. He seemed to relate well to his environment and to other people. Hallucinations disappeared, and his emotionality toned down, appearing to become harmonious with his thoughts and his situation, His conversation seemed to be freer and more spontaneous. His words flowed more smoothly and with fewer signs of blocking. Signs of obsessional thinking were lost and there appeared to be less self-preoccupation.

These records are interesting in two respects. First, they show how the "improvement" following surgery may be accompanied by other changes which, under careful scrutiny, do not appear to be altogether healthy. Second, they offer a welcome bit of validation for the sentence completion method itself. In 1951, Jenkins and Holsopple reported, after examination of a very small sample of sentence completions from lobotomized patients, that "the shift in the Sentence Completion from preoperative to three-month postoperative is a type of shift suggesting reduction of internal conflict, reduction of extent or com-

plexity of feeling-quality, reduction of awareness of and
sensitivity to feelings of others, reduction of concern with
or responsiveness to moral scruples or other acquired internal controls. The new orientation is an emotionally un-
responsive, extroverted, practical, laconically expressed
"realism" which does not take the world too seriously—
perhaps sometimes not seriously enough."

This characterization appears to fit neatly these more
recent records. The preoperative responses are in the
left hand column, the postoperative in the right.

1. *Children are usually certain that*
   Their parents are right.   What they do will be repaid.

2. *People are praised when*
   They   have   done   well.   They do well.

3. *A large crowd*
   Is very interesting.   Gathered.

4. *A person is most helpless when*
   He has given up.   Immovable.

5. *When an animal is wild*
   He is uncontrolled.   He's lucky.

6. *The hardest decisions*
   Are most important ones.   Are best.

7. *The easiest way to get money*
   Is not always best.   Win it.

8. *Twenty years from now*
   Things will be different.   —Who knows?

9. *Parents would worry less if*
   Everthing were well with   Sure.
   their children.

10. *When fire starts*
    It must be controlled.   —Stop it.

11. *Compared with dogs, cats are*
    Light and quick.   Smaller.

12. *Fathers should learn that*
    The hard ways for them   And more.
    is sometimes right.

13. *One's closest friends can*
    Be almost a necessity.   Do one.

14. *It is easy to get into trouble when*
    Things seem smoothest.   Today.

15. *Few children fear*
    Something unknown.   The unknown.

16. *At the end of the road*
    —the ocean.   Don't worry.

17. *He drew back from the touch of*
    A stranger.   Her.

18. *The white girl who married the colored man*
    Regretted it.   Regretted it.

19. *The most pleasant dreams*
    Are short and intense.   Are fleeting,

20. *A drunken man*
    May do strange things.   Is unresponsible.

21. *No one can repair the damage caused by*
    Atomic action.   Atomic explosion.

22. *The nicest thing about being a child*
    Is complete faith and in- Is freedom.
    nocence.

23. *There is hardly any*
    Unfairness in a child's na- More.
    ture.

24. *To be without shame*
    Is to be happy.   Is good.

25. *Worse than being lonely is*
    To be with wrong associ-   Too much company.
    ates.

26. *When a person is ill*
    He should see a doctor.   Cure him.

27. *A man can stop beating his wife only if*
    She deserves it.   Apart.

28. *The best thing about old age*
    Is knowing answers.   Is others.

29. *Children are most annoying when*
    Not understood.   At a certain age.

30. *If people only knew how much*
    Their time is worth.   Is plenty.

31. *The main difference between a wild and a tame animal is*
    Habits and strength.   Environment.

32. *Few things are less attractive than*
    A woman who is trying
    hardest to be.

33. *The worst thing about being sick*
    Is the things missed out   Is getting cured.
    on.

34. *It is often hard to sleep when*
    It is noisy.   Alone.

35. *People shouldn't*
    Judge others entirely by   Think of it.
    appearance.

36. *To be a good liar one must*
    Be a fisherman. (No tales   Practice.
    harmful to others.)

37. *A masculine woman should*
    Cultivate men.   Develop the feminine.

38. *People refrain from murder only because*
Of the consequences.   Observed.

39. *Too much distance lies between*
Types of people.   Us.

40. *The best of mothers may forget that*
Childrens thoughts are at   And also this.
times adult.

41. *There ought to be a law to*
Prevent such things.   Stop it.

42. *Spiders are*
At the center of webs.   Busybodies.

43. *When a criminal leaves the prison he*
Starts new.   Starts new.

44. *Compared with sisters brothers are*
Equal.   More active.

45. *The finger pointed*
And the sign was stop.   Up.

46. *Children are least annoying when*
Happiest.   Asleep.

47. *To avoid a fight one must*
Break rules of nature.   Disregard causes.

48. *A naked man*
Is free in movement.   In Borneo.

49. *Closer and closer there comes*
The dawn.   Tomorrow.

50. *There would be more divorces if*
People followed only their   There were more marriages.
desires.

51. *A drunken woman*
Should be helped.   Needs help.

52. *When a person is wounded*
Quickest attention is best.   He may be cured.

53. *One's best friend may be irritating when*
They disagree.   With him.

54. *A woman's body*
Sure is something.

55. *A weak person does not often*
Get the best result.   Win.

56. *Down underground*
Are coal, oil, iron, copper   Could be anything.
and numerous supplies.

57. *One can hardly see*
Until he looks carefully.   Why it is allowed.

58. *Wouldn't it be really funny if*
Things   result   as   our   Our son strip-teased for the —?
dreams.

59. *The kind of animal I would like most to be*
Man.   Man.

60. *Nothing is harder to stop than*
Custom.   An argument.

61. *The two most beautiful things I have ever seen*
A woman and a waterfall.   My mother and—

62. *She couldn't bear to touch*
Him.   It.

63. *A woman who has lost her virtue must*
Look carefully for others.   Improvise.

64. *Failure may be expected when*
Faith is not present.   Due.

65. *An effeminate man may*
Be avoided.   Accent the masculine.

66. *It hurts when*
    It reaches your con-   Realized.
    science.

67. *The deeper one goes*
    The more he finds.   The more he finds.

68. *Behind one's back*
    Anything may happen.   Irrelivent.

69. *When the car skidded*
    He accelerated and it   My heart caused a woosh in the
    caught again.   throat.

70. *A mother is more likely than a father to*
    Foretell something bad. Forgive.

71. *The worst kind of criminal*
    May be cured.   May be bettered.

72. *If one cannot own*
    Something it may be pos- One might copy.
    sible to lease it.

73. *Tests like this*
    Are puzzling.   Are used.

3. DAISY AND ELOISE

Daisy and Eloise are 21-year-old identical twins, hospitalized, both with a diagnosis of paranoid schizophrenia. The first pair of records were obtained shortly after admission, the second pair several months later. In the interval Daisy had been discharged and was receiving outpatient psychotherapy. Eloise, who appeared the more disturbed of the two, continued in the hospital with both insulin shock and psychotherapy. At the time of the second record Eloise was considered to be in an acutely disturbed state, Daisy to be making a fair social adjustment.

Two contrasts are apparent in the records, that between Daisy and Eloise at the time of admission, and the difference in the kind of change shown by each of the patients.

Daisy 1	*Eloise 1*

1. *Children are usually certain that*

Grown-ups do not know what is best for them.	Smiles from their parents mean they are feeling well.

2. *People are praised when*

They have accomplished a difficult feat.	They are courageous.

3. *A large crowd*

Watched the parade.	Usually gathers when celebrities appear.

4. *A person is most helpless when*

He or she is ill emotionally.	He is mentally ill.

5. *When an animal is wild*

It is dangerous.	He may attack human beings.

6. *The hardest decisions*

Are the ones you must make when you are emotionally ill and are afraid of making a mistake.	To make are when you are mentally sick.

7. *The easiest way to get money*

Is to work for it yourself and not depend on anyone else.	Is to work well.

8. *Twenty years from now*

I hope doctors will have better methods.	Ought to bring forth some treatment to get me well.

9. *Parents would worry less if*

They were emotionally stable themselves and their children were too.	They were emotionally stable and mature themselves.

10. *When fire starts*

The first thing you must do is keep calm so you can think straight.   The fire department should be immediately notified.

11. *Compared with dogs, cats are*

Also pets which you can enjoy or which you can dislike, depending on which you prefer.   Less dangerous.

12. *Fathers should learn that*

If a child is not emotionally well, it is not that the child wants to be that way or that it is lazy.   Their daughters can be trusted.

13. *One's closest friends can*

Not always understand about mental illness, so it is best not to tell them about it.   Misunderstand you if you are ill.

14. *It is easy to get into trouble when*

You are all mixed up emotionally.   A person has been insane.

15. *Few children fear*

Mental disorders when they're young.   Kind and loving parents.

16. *At the end of the road*

Of life, which is death, comes lasting peace for there is no such thing as hell, except when life itself becomes that.   Was the river.

17. *He drew back from the touch of*

The hand of fear.   An ugly and depressed woman.

18. *The white girl who married the colored man*

Probably was very mixed up emotionally.   Was said to be emotionally unstable.

19. *The most pleasant dreams*

Are the ones which you have when you are mentally well, for you don't have pleasant ones when you're not.

Are dreams I seldom have.

20. *A drunken man*

Is usually that way because he tried to escape something which is pressing on his mind.

Is a sick individual and should be recognized as such.

21. *No one can repair the damage caused by*

Doctors who refuse to consider but one method of treatment for a patient and continue to make the patient think it is the only good method when it doesn't help the patient.

Mentally sick people who mistreat timid people so that they can release their tension and hostility.

22. *The nicest thing about being a child*

Is if you are a normal one—I never enjoyed childhood too much.

(I do not feel there in anything nice about being a child.)

23. *There is hardly any*

Thing worse than a mental disorder.

Treatment I feel can help me to get well.

24. *To be without shame*

Is to be well emotionally and not pick on yourself for what mistakes you think you have made—also it might mean you're sick emotionally and are defying certain laws humanity has made.

Indicates that a person doesn't punish himself.

25. *Worse than being lonely is*

Being depressed and filled with fear, not only about the present, but even worse, your whole life.

Being depressed and mentally tired.

26. *When a person is ill*

That is mentally, he isn't necessarily that way because he unsconscientiously wants to be that way.

Mentally, there is little chance of his getting well.

27. *A man can stop beating his wife only if*

He is cured of what is bothering him emotionally.

He realizes he is sick and seeks treatment.

28. *The best thing about old age*

Is when you can enjoy it and look back on a fruitful life.

Is the thought that I'd soon be dead.

29. *Children are most annoying when*

You yourself are mentally ill.

When I am feeling sick and cannot love them.

30. *If people only knew how much*

People suffer from mental illnesses, they might do more about it and contribute more for research than they do.

Depressed people suffer, they would try to develop more treatment to get them well.

31. *The main difference between a wild and tame animal is*

The way they're constructed and also training but even with training a wild animal may become dangerous because of some circumstance.

That one is hated and feared, while the other is usually trusted and loved.

32. *Few things are less attractive than*

Being mentally ill.

A person who looks depressed and anxious all the time.

33. *The worst thing about being sick*

(Inserted "mentally" before sick) Is not to be cured and thinking you must spend the rest of your life that way.

Mentally is that I want to get well but cannot seem to snap out of it.

34. *It is often hard to sleep when*

You are emotionally ill and have to think of waking up in fear.

My mind is troubled and I detest the thought of waking up in the morning.

35. *People shouldn't*

Try to offer advice to sick people when they don't really know much about the illness; they only make the person feel worse.

Think a person is inferior because he may be of a different race, religion, or nationality than their own.

36. *To be a good liar one must*

Not only fool others, but fool himself too.

Have confidence in himself and not be afraid of what others might think.

37. *A masculine woman should*

See a psychiatrist to help her find out what is making her that way.

Be happy as she seems to be unafraid and walk with confidence as a man does.

38. *People refrain from murder only because*

Their minds keep them from doing it, because of punishment by the law or self-punishment or because they simply have no thoughts of wanting to murder.

Their primitive impulses have been repressed.

39. *Too much distance lies between*

Being sick and being well emotionally, so that people who are well, do not know how a sick person needs help.

My mind and the minds of others.

40. *The best of mothers may forget that*

If a child is too good, it is not normal.

Children should be taught to love and trust everyone, no matter how different they may be from themselves.

41. *There ought to be a law to*

Provide much more aid to mental hospitals and much more aid for mental research.

Increase the number of mental hospitals and increase the research in the treatment of mental illness.

42. *Spiders are*

Ugly and if I never see a real one, I won't care.

Ugly animals which make me sick.

43. *When a criminal leaves the prison he*

Is not always cured of what made him commit the crime in the first place and may go out and do the same thing again.

Should try to start a new and better life for himself and other people should do their best to help him.

44. *Compared with sisters brothers are*

Just the opposite sex and can be just as emotional.

Lucky because they are usually loved more by parents and are allowed more privileges; therefore, they are taught to feel superior.

45. *The finger pointed*

Is considered by some people to be a wrong thing to do.

By prejudiced people at a foreigner is something I detest.

46. *Children are least annoying when*

You are in a contented frame of mind yourself.

I am feeling well.

47. *To avoid a fight one must*

Keep control of himself.

Keep quiet.

48. *A naked man*

Can seem like something disgusting to a girl or woman who thinks sex is dirty.

Is very happy when sleeping with a woman

49. *Closer and closer there comes*

The time when more and more people with mental disorders can be helped.

To people in this country the fear that we'll always be in a war and never enjoy complete peace.

50. *There would be more divorces if*

Roman Catholics were allowed to divorce and if divorce lows were more lenient in some states.

Contraception were used by married people and they had no children to think of if they wanted a divorce.

51. *A drunken woman*

Is usually considered worse than a drunken man, but they're both sick people if they do it continually.

Is hated more than a drunken man; therefore, I myself feel sorry for her.

52. *When a person is wounded*

It is not always physically.

Physically, he does not have to punish himself as a person who is mentally ill.

53. *One's best friend may be irritating when*

A person is irritated himself.

You are feeling depressed and nervous.

54. *A woman's body*

Is so constructed so as to bear children.

Should not be permitted to get fat.

55. *A weak person does not often*

Want to be that way—
everyone would like to be
brave.

Want to live because he may hate
himself for not being strong.

56. *Down underground*

Dead people are buried,
but no one knows what, if
anything happens after
death.

Is where dead people (who I regard as lucky individuals) are
buried.

57. *One can hardly see*

How much a person may
be suffering just by looking at the person.

The prejudice and discrimination
practiced in this country.

58. *Wouldn't it be really funny if*

If people who make fun
of mentally sick people had
a taste of mental illness
themselves, even though
I'd hate to wish it on anyone.

I were to get well?

59. *The kind of animal I would like most to be*

Would not be any except
human being.

A little puppy dog because he is
so lovable and seems to be able
to return the love that is given to
him.

60. *Nothing is harder to stop than*

Trying to stop your own
fears and depressions yourself.

Chronic depression and mental
fatigue.

61. *The two most beautiful things I have ever seen*

Are difficult to say. Life
itself is the most beautiful
thing when you are hap-
py, and everything about
it can seem beautiful.

62. *She couldn't bear to touch*

Her own sex organs, think-   A man's body.
ing sex was disgusting.

63. *A woman who has lost her virtue must*

Not make herself miser-   Try very—all she can to regain it
able the rest of her life,   and prove to other people that
because she had.   she has regained it.

64. *Failure may be expected when*

Something is not done the   A person is pessimistic, hates
right way or when some-   himself, and cannot think clearly.
one is conditioned to fail-
ure in the first place.

65. *An effeminate man may*

Be that way because of   Not be able to receive treatment.
an emotional reason and
should seek help.

66. *It hurts when*

You hear people making   I want to love people and be like
fun of others who are   them, but cannot.
mentally ill.

67. *The deeper one goes*

Into psychiatry, the more   With psychoanalysis, the worse
he knows. Some people   one may become if you are not
think you know less.   suited for that type of treatment.

68. *Behind one's back*

Is nothing to fear unless   People may talk against you, yet
the person imagines it.   compliment you when facing you.

69. *When the car skidded*

The man kept calm and   Off the road, it was because the
did the right things to stop   driver had not been concentrating
the car from continuing to   on the driving.
skid.

70. *A mother is more likely than a father to*

Worry about her children and blame herself if something happens to her children.   Love her children.

71. *The worst kind of criminal*

Is a person who takes advantage of other human beings.   Is one who is mentally sane.

72. *If one cannot own*

Something by working for it, he should not steal it.   A house, I consider him unlucky.

73. *Tests like this*

Take quite some time to finish but I hope this test is helpful.   Are very boring and do not seem to accomplish much in order to help me to get well.

Daisy 2	*Eloise* 2

1. *Children are usually certain that*

Whatever they do is correct.   They do not have to worry as much as older people.

2. *People are praised when*

They have performed a job well done.   They are attractive, intelligent, and love other people.

3. *A large crowd*

If swayed the wrong way, can be a dangerous thing.   Gets me frightened and upset.

4. *A person is most helpless when*

He is emotionally insecure.   He is mentally sick.

5. *When an animal is wild*

Keep out of its way.   I get frantic and fear the worst.

6. *The hardest decisions*

Should always be sought with intelligence before being made.   To make are when I feel depressed and disturbed.

7. *The easiest way to get money*

Is to work for it.   Is to become a psychiatrist or government employee.

8. *Twenty years from now*

Either all nations must have learned to live with each other and, if not, may perish.   Perhaps psychiatrists will know how to cure mental patients.

9. *Parents would worry less if*

They were emotionally secure themselves and used common sense before worrying needlessly.   They were mentally well themselves.

10. *When fire starts*

You must remain calm and composed so you'll know the proper steps to take.   I become extremely frightened and want to run away.

11. *Compared with dogs, cats are*

Not as popular.   Ugly and cannot be loved as much.

12. *Fathers should learn that*

Punishing a child is only going to make matters worse.   Children need love and understand you.

13. *One's closest friends can*

At times appear to turn against you—usually you'll realize it is not your friend who has changed.   Hurt you or turn against you.

14. *It is easy to get into trouble when*

You are insecure and therefore try to solve your problems in a childish frame of mind.   One starts taking narcotics or alcohol.

15. *Few children fear*
     The state of world affairs.   Life if they have had a happy
                                     childhood.

16. *At the end of the road*
     In life, there is no turning   Are usually bars.
     back.

17. *He drew back from the touch of*
     Fear.   The man who was feminine.

18. *The white girl who married the colored man*
     Was not a well adjusted   Should have seen a psychiatrist
     person.   as she was not well.

19. *The most pleasant dreams*
     Are the ones that produce   Are those where I am loved and
     action—otherwise, dreams   feel confident.
     are worthless.

20. *A drunken man*
     Is usually a man trying   Is mentally unhappy and is seek-
     to run away from his prob-   ing an escape from his troubles.
     lems

21. *No one can repair the damage caused by*
     Useless thinking.   Parents who teach their children
                                    to fear and hurt people.

22. *The nicest thing about being a child*
     Is if you are a happy one.   (I am unable to answer this as I
                                    was never a happy child.)

23. *There is hardly any*
     Use worrying about the   Good cures for mental illness.
     past.

24. *To be without shame*
     Is necessarily an asset.   Appears impossible for me.

25. *Worse than being lonely is*
     Never trying to find out   When I hate myself and am afraid
     why you are.   of my thoughts.

26. *When a person is ill*

Emotionally, sympathy will not do any good.　It usually stems from mental rather than physical reasons.

27. *A man can stop beating his wife only if*

He wants to　He is mentally well.

28. *The best thing about old age*

Not regretting it.　Is that one can look forward to death.

29. *Children are most annoying when*

We are annoyed ourselves and expect too much of them.　I do not feel well.

30. *If people only knew how much*

A little understanding of others means instead of petty gossip, they would learn to love others.　I want to love them, they would not regard me as being a cold-hearted person.

31. *The main difference between a wild and a tame animal is*

That one is hated while the other is loved.

32. *Few things are less attractive than*

A person who gossips.　A girl who hates herself and thinks she is unattractive.

33. *The worst thing about being sick*

Is not doing anything about it.　Is hating myself and being depressed.

34. *It is often hard to sleep when*

You have feelings of guilt.　My sister is out with men and I become envious of her.

35. *People shouldn't*

Degrade others, for we're all human beings.　Be so mentally confused.

36. *To be a good liar one must*
    Deceive himself too.   Become a psychiatrist.

37. *A masculine woman should*
    Realize that she's neither   Kill herself.
    well liked by men or wo-
    men.

38. *People refrain from murder only because*
    They're afraid.   They are afraid of their con-
                                 sciences and also of being caught.

39. *Too much distance lies between*
    What we know we should   My mind and the minds of other
    do and what we do do.   people.

40. *The best of mothers may forget that*
    Children are children and   Children are sensitive and need
    need time to grow up.   confidence.

41. *There ought to be a law to*
    Be kind to others and not   Carry on more research in the
    gossip.   field of psychiatry.

42. *Spiders are*
    Creepy looking things.   Ugly and dreadful.

43. *When a criminal leaves the prison he*
    May be worse than when   May find it difficult to start a new
    he went in.   life.

44. *Compared with sisters brothers are*
    Just the opposite sex.   Extremely lucky and usually con-
                                 sider themselves so.

45. *The finger pointed*
    Accusingly at the person.   At me makes me nervous and
                                 afraid.

46. *Children are least annoying when*
    They're asleep.   I feel well and have a love for
                                 life.

47. *To avoid a fight one must*

Use his intelligence and not his emotions.   Remind himself that love accomplishes more than hate.

48. *A naked man*

Is naked for some reason.   Likes to sleep with a woman.

49. *Closer and closer there comes*

The time when.   A love for my psychiatrist and I feel afraid of it.

50. *There would be more divorces if*

They were easier to get and no alimony to pay.   All mentally ill persons got married.

51. *A drunken woman*

Looks worse than a drunken man.   Is to be pitied as she is seeking the wrong type of escape from life.

52. *When a person is wounded*

In his feelings, it is the worst kind of wound.   I feel happy.

53. *One's best friend may be irritating when*

You yourself are irritated.   You are disturbed.

54. *A woman's body*

Is made that way to bear children.   Is interesting to look at if the woman is naked and looks like me.

55. *A weak person does not often*

Like to admit it to himself.   Have confidence in himself.

56. *Down underground*

Is more earth.   Are rats, worms, and other disgusting creatures.

57. *One can hardly see*

What is true if he is not in a calm frame of mind.   I am a sexy woman as I do not show it.

58. *Wouldn't it be really funny if*

Some people knew how   I attacked a man.
silly they act.

59. *The kind of animal I would like most to be*

Don't care to be anything   Is a lion because then I could be
but a human being.   master of other people.

60. *Nothing is harder to stop than*

Propaganda when people   Anxiety, depression, and hatred
want to believe it.   of oneself.

61. *The two most beautiful things I have ever seen*

Are not capable of being   Were seen after I came out of in-
purchased.   sulin coma.

62. *She couldn't bear to touch*

The fellow she disliked.   A man's body as she was afraid of
sex.

63. *A woman who has lost her virtue must*

Understand why she has   Be mentally sick.
and resolve to solve her
problems in a better way.

64. *Failure may be expected when*

You go about things in the   You wish for it, as I unfortunately
wrong way.   do sometimes.

65. *An effeminate man may*

(I need a dictionary.)

66. *It hurts when*

You've hurt someone dear   I hate myself and have no faith
to you.   in God or my doctor.

67. *The deeper one goes*

Into human nature, the   Into psychotherapy, the more he
wiser he becomes.   may get disturbed temporarily.

68. *Behind one's back*

Is nothing, if you're not   Are no sex organs.
afraid.

69. *When the car skidded*
    It could only be brought   I became afraid and nervous.
    back into control by clear
    thinking and quick action.

70. *A mother is more likely than a father to*
    Be around it's child more.   Love her children.

71. *The worst kind of criminal*
    Has some good in him, no   Is one who does not have a con-
    matter how it is repressed.   science.

72. *If one cannot own*
    Something, he can work   Any money, I feel sorry for him.
    for it.

73. *Tests like this*
    Are tedious when you're   Make me laugh.
    worrying about something.

Evidence for the diagnosis of paranoid schizophrenia is abundantly clear in the sentence completion material and it seems more useful to discuss the records comparatively than to point out the correspondence between them and classic descriptions of paranoid schizophrenia.

In comparing the initial records of the two sisters, one is immediately struck with the large number of responses which are closely similar. However, Daisy is relatively flat, superficial and depressed. Eloise appears more active, agitated and alive. Refer to sentences 10, 23, 28, 31, 36, 44, 45, 51, 59, 64, 66, 68, 69, 73.

Comparison of the later records, with reference to the initial ones, strongly suggests that an inference concerning severity of illness drawn from the fact of hospitalization may be of doubtful value. The patient's resignation to the schizophrenic process does not necessarily interfere with social adjustment, whereas the efforts of the patient to come to grips with her problems may in themselves lead to estimates of poor social adjustment. Daisy's second record, although admittedly less depressed, is even flatter and more superficial. This is not concealed by its greater conformity to conventional verbal stereotypes. Eloise is more disturbed, more aggressive, but her problems are real ones and she is trying to meet them. See sentences 2, 6, 7, 10, 14, 15, 21, 23, 24, etc., in Daisy's first and second records, and sentences 3, 5, 7, 10, 19, 30, 34, etc., in Eloise's.

4. FLORA

Flora is a 60-year-old married woman with a history of 40 years of periods of mania, depression, and remission. The manic and depressive periods have grown in intensity and duration in recent years. Both records were obtained in a mental hospital, the first during a manic attack, shortly after its peak, the second two months later, in remission. During the two months' hospitalization she received three electroshock treatments. The first record appears in the left column, the second in the right. The second record, with its paucity of responses, should not be considered as unproductive as the comparison may suggest. The first was given orally, the second Flora wrote herself.

First record

Second record

1. *Children are usually certain that*
   Father and mother should know best—no, you have to learn that by experience—papa and mama care for me.

   Parents care for them.

2. *People are praised when*
   They do things in a cheerful mood.

   They do good work.

3. *A large crowd*
   Of folks show you have friends.

   Always gathers if they hear a strange noise.

4. *A person is most helpless when*
   Down in spirits.   Scared.

5. *When an animal is wild*
   It needs correction.   Leave it alone.

6. *The hardest decisions*
   Are those made by your-   To make are for other folks.
   self.

7. *The easiest way to get money*
   Is to take it—but honestly. Is to work for it.

8. *Twenty years from now*
   It will be 1972.

9. *Parents would worry less if*
   Children obeyed their
   parents.

10. *When fire starts*
    Leave it alone—or try to   Call the fire engine.
    help if necessary to outten
    it.

11. *Compared with dogs, cats are*
    More cunning, quicker.   More playful.

12. *Fathers should learn that*
    To have a home happy, it
    requires mutual under-
    standing by both parties—
    a life of give and take.

13. *One's closest friends can*
    Not be numbered.   Not always give advice.

14. *It is easy to get into trouble when*
    You don't mind your own   One is not busy with work.
    affairs.

15. *Few children fear*
    Their father.

16. *At the end of the road*
    You must look which way
    to go or turn back—turn
    back or stop—turn back
    because you can't stop
    forever—they'll push you
    around.

17. *He drew back from the touch of*
    The master's hand.

18. *The white girl who married the colored man*
    Caused the intermingling
    of relationship.

19. *The most pleasant dreams*
    Are day dreams—when   Are soon forgotten.
    your mind is working in
    a normal condition.

20. *A drunken man*
    Is not sensible.   Should never drive a car.

21. *No one can repair the damage caused by*
    An unbalanced mind.

22. *The nicest thing about being a child*
    Is innocence.   Is being innocent.

23. *There is hardly any*
    Human being born per-
    fect.

24. *To be without shame*
    Has been the downfall of   Will cause shame
    our creation.

25. *Worse than being lonely is*
    Companionship with peo-   To be sick.
    ple who don't have
    enough work to do.

26. *When a person is ill*
    Rest is needed.   They should consult a doctor.

27. *A man can stop beating his wife only if*
Strength fails.

28. *The best thing about old age*
A hoary head is a crown
of glory.

29. *Children are most annoying when*
Teased.   Asking many questions.

30. *If people only knew how much*
A child means in this
world, they would stop to
realize they were children
too at one time.

31. *The main difference between a wild and a tame animal is*
Education or training.   The tame one was trained.

32. *Few things are less attractive than*
Nature.

33. *The worst thing about being sick*
Is to rebuild the human   Is to get well.
body.

34. *It is often hard to sleep when*
Unbalanced.   You are not sleepy.

35. *People shouldn't*
Try to tantalize—try to   Always express their thoughts.
disturb.

36. *To be a good liar one must*
Have been doing it quite   Tell many falsehoods.
a while.

37. *A masculine woman should*
Do more work, manual
work.

38. *People refrain from murder only because*
Of the punishment they
get for murdering some-
one.

39. *Too much distance lies between*
Love and death, or life
and death.

40. *The best of mothers may forget that*
It was God's plan to have   They were children also.
her help create the com-
ing generation.

41. *There ought to be a law to*
Teach man to respect his
family, his country, his
neighbor, or to use the
Golden Rule.

42. *Spiders are*
Creatures that spin a web.

43. *When a criminal leaves the prison he*
Must turn a new leaf and   Is free.
mend his ways or suffer
the consequences over
again.

44. *Compared with sisters brothers are*
The stronger.   Usually stronger.

45. *The finger pointed*
Is scornful.   To the name of the street.

46. *Children are least annoying when*
Happy.   They have something to do.

47. *To avoid a fight one must*
Pull away from it—walk out.

48. *A naked man*
Is God's creation, God's
plan.

49. *Closer and closer there comes*
Loneliness.

50. *There would be more divorces if*
It were not for the law of
love.

51. *A drunken woman*
Has no sane mind.

52. *When a person is wounded*
He needs rest or rebuild-
ing his body.

53. *One's best friend may be irritating when*
Under a nervous strain.

54. *A woman's body*
Is God's plan of creation.

55. *A weak person does not often*
Need sympathy. Care for too much exercise.

56. *Down underground*
There lies the law of gravi- Are many streams of water.
ty.

57. *One can hardly see*
Through God's plan of In the dark.
creation.

58. *Wouldn't it be really funny if*
God had not planted into
human beings a mind, a
brain.

59. *The kind of animal I would like most to be*
Is what I am.

60. *Nothing is harder to stop than*
Man's tongue—you can put A false story.
a bridle on a horse's
mouth.

61. *The two most beautiful things I have ever seen*
    Are nature — that's not   Were sunshine and flowers.
    two—Yes, it would be two.

62. *She couldn't bear to touch*
    Her wounded husband.

63. *A woman who has lost her virtue must*
    Try to be cheerful and
    give cheer.

64. *Failure may be expected when*
    You look forward to suc-   Least looks for it.
    cess or to succeed.

65. *An effeminate man may*
    Be very unkind, unknow-
    ingly, to all he meets.

66. *It hurts when*
    Being misunderstood.   Folks talk unkind about you.

67. *The deeper one goes*
    The more work it requires.

68. *Behind one's back*
    Is very trying in many
    ways to a traitor.

69. *When the car skidded*
    It jumped.   It caused the accident.

70. *A mother is more likely than a father to*
    Be affected there—to suf-
    fer the consequences.

71. *The worst kind of criminal*
    Is not law-abiding.

72. *If one cannot own*
    At least one may share.

73. *Tests like this*
    Are hard to hear.   Are not easily answered.

In Flora's first record, her first sentence (Children are usually certain that / father and mother should know best—no, you have to learn that by experience—papa and mama care for me) contains many of the factors which characterize the total picture. Conflict about authority appears, mental confusion is present, as is a tendency to flight of ideas, and, perhaps most striking, there is her extreme dependence. She seems to identify with a young child.

The record contains a mixture of both manic and depressive features. In fact a quick reading of the record is perhaps likely to suggest that the subject is in an agitated depression rather than in a manic state. It is as though the mania is a frantic fight against the depression rather than a successful escape from it. The completions suggest that for Flora both her depression and her mania serve similar functions: the expression of an insoluble conflict between her rebellion against authority (and against masculinity, which she equates with authority) and her tremendous need for its support:

"38. People refrain from murder only because / of the punishment they get for murdering someone.

41. There ought to be a law to / teach man to respect his family, his country, his neighbor, or to use the Golden Rule.

50. There would be more divorces if / it were not for the law of love.

62. She couldn't bear to touch / her wounded husband."

The conflict leads to intense feelings of guilt, and the recurring phases of her disease seem to represent her attempt to escape punishment for her rebellion and hostility:

"47. To avoid a fight one must / pull away from it— walk out."

Despite the meagerness of the second record (a qualitative as well as a quantitative meagerness), the improvement is impressive. The confusion in thinking has cleared, the perseverative delusional ideas have disappeared, the orientation is realistic and appropriate. There is no indication, of course, that any basic problem has been solved. The fact that this period of calm is also part of her stormy cycle is well symbolized in her completion of No. 24 in the second record: "To be without shame / will cause shame."

5. GEORGE

George is nine years old. He is clearly of superior intelligence. His record and those of Irene and Jeremy are included in order to show that psychological techniques which commonly highlight the drab, unpleasant, and unhappy aspects of personality may equally well differentiate among varieties of healthy people and even while pointing toward their weaknesses may bring out their attractive and strong properties.

1. *Children are usually certain that*

    they are liked.

2. *People are praised when*

    they do something approved of.

3. *A large crowd*

    is waiting for a bus.

4. *A person is most helpless when*

    he is tied.

5. *When an animal is wild*

    he is fierce.

6. *The hardest decisions*

are not always as hard as you think.

7. *The easiest way to get money*

to inherit.

8. *Twenty years from now*

I hope to be married and have a family.

9. *Parents would worry less if*

their children were more responsible.

10. *When fire starts*

there is usually panic.

11. *Compared with dogs, cats are*

sometimes more friendly, sometimes less friendly.

12. *Fathers should learn that*

their children admire them.

13. *One's closest friends can*

often cheer one up.

14. *It is easy to get into trouble when*

one starts a fight.

15. *Few children fear*

their friends.

16. *At the end of the road*

lies the forest.

17. *He drew back from the touch of*

fire.

18. *The white girl who married the colored man*

lived and were happy.

19. *The most pleasant dreams*

are ones you do not remember.

20. *A drunken man*

yelled to his friend.

21. *No one can repair the damage caused by*

That's hard—a man. Doesn't have to be—just an answer.

22. *The nicest thing about being a child*

> you don't have to worry about working.

23. *There is hardly any*

> hatred.

24. *To be without shame*

> be happy.

25. *Worse than being lonely is*

> being friendless.

26. *When a person is ill*

> he is in bed.

27. *A man can stop beating his wife only if*

> he gets sober.

28. *The best thing about old age*

> social security.

29. *Children are most annoying when*

> (Laugh) I'd rather not give that one—they are sick, "Get me this, get me that."

30. *If people only knew how much*

> talking disturbed me, they would stop.

31. *The main difference between a wild and a tame animal is*

> one is sometimes not friendly but the other is.

32. *Few things are less attractive than*

> a drunken man.

33. *The worst thing about being sick*

> you may not get up.

34. *It is often hard to sleep when*

> Christmas is tomorrow.

35. *People shouldn't*

> talk so much.

36. *To be a good liar one must*

> not tell the truth.

37. *A masculine woman should*

> be feminine.

38. *People refrain from murder only because*
> it is not in them.

39. *Too much distance lies between*
> here and there.

40. *The best of mothers may forget that*
> they are their child's best friend.

41. *There ought to be a law to*
> not have jaywalkers.

42. *Spiders are*
> eight-legged.

43. *When a criminal leaves the prison he*
> feels happy.

44. *Compared with sisters, brothers are*
> more active.

45. *The finger pointed*
> north.

46. *Children are least annoying when*
> they are asleep.

47. *To avoid a fight one must*
> keep to himself.

48. *A naked man*
> puts on his clothes.

49. *Closer and closer there comes*
> Louie.

50. *There would be more divorces if*
> it were cheaper.

51. *A drunken woman*
> has drunk punch.

52. *When a person is wounded*
> he is helpless.

53. *One's best friend may be irritating when*
> he does not give in to you.

54. *A woman's body*
> lies in the coffin.

55. *A weak person does not often*
> fight.

56. *Down underground*
> Pluto.

57. *One can hardly see*

     down underground.

58. *Wouldn't it be really funny if*

     you were me—if I were
     you.

59. *The kind of animal I would like most to be*

     a baby chihuahua.

60. *Nothing is harder to stop than*

     the falling rock.

61. *The two most beautiful things I have ever seen*

     him and her.

62. *She couldn't bear to touch*

     the flaming building.

63. *(Not given.)*

64. *(Not given.)*

65. *An effeminate man may*

     want to be masculine.

66. *It hurts when*

     I was alone.

67. *The deeper one goes*

     downward, he falls.

68. *Behind one's back*

     he doesn't know what happens.

69. *When the car skidded*

     it came down the hill.

70. *A mother is more likely than a father to*

     get worried.

71. *The worst kind of criminal*

     is never all bad.

72. *If one cannot own*

     it, he borrowed it.

73. *Tests like this*

     are sometimes useful—but
     you get rather bored toward
     the end of it.

No one could call this intelligent youngster "relaxed."

"4. A person is most helpless when / he is tied.

5. When an animal is wild / he is fierce."

Nor could one reasonably call him more tense than an only child of superior parents might be expected to be.

"13. One's closest friends can / often cheer one up.

25. Worse than being lonely is / being friendless.

6. The hardest decisions / are not always as hard as you think."

Certainly there is resentment against adult authority, and a normal nine-year-old feeling that he is being "pushed around."

"12. Fathers should learn that / their children admire them.

40. The best of mothers may forget that / they are their child's best friend."

At the same time he shows the trust and confidence in adults that every parent hopes to see.

"22. The nicest thing about being a child / you don't have to worry about working.

29. Children are most annoying when / (laugh) I'd rather not give that one—

58. (Response to adult examiner) Wouldn't it be really funny if / you were me—if I were you."

If in this record one finds the normal anxiety, tensions, and rebellion of an only child, he also sees the resources with which the youngster meets his issues: friendliness, responsibility, dependability, high motivation, flexibility, and humor.

6. HENRY

Henry is a nine-year-old boy, and something of a problem. He has a protective but often annoyed older brother and a highly competitive younger sister. He has always expressed a frank dislike for women. Life, for him, is a constant battle. In meeting competition his ethics and morals sometimes appear to be rather immature—even for a nine year old. There is not the least doubt that he wants to be a "big shot" nor that he wants desperately to be loved and knows that he often makes a mess of it. The first 16 completions were written by the boy but it was such a painful job that the rest of the sentences were given orally. Sentences which were not given or which elicited no response are omitted.

In this record several repetitive completions stand out.

"17. He drew back from the touch of / a fist.
21. No one can repair the damage caused by / my fist.
47. To avoid a fight one must / sock the other guy.
53. One's best friend may be irritating when / he starts punching you.
55. A weak person does not often / keep from fighting."

But physical combat does not always result in victory:

4. "A person is most helpless when / he is tied.
19. The most pleasant dreams / are horrible.
25. Worse than being lonely is / being socked in the nose."

And the consequence:

68. "Behind one's back / I can do anything but in front on one's back I can't do anything."

3. *A large crowd*

is very annoying.

4. *A person is most helpless when*

he is tied.

5. *When an animal is wild*

it is tame.

6. *The hardest decisions*

are made by umpires.

7. *The easiest way to get money*

is to steal it.

8. *Twenty years from now*

I'll be 29.

10. *When fire starts*

put it out.

11. *Compared with dogs, cats are*

dopes.

12. *Fathers should learn that*

"Henry" is a good name.

14. *It is easy to get into trouble when*

when you are bad.

15. *Few children fear*

lions.

16. *At the end of the road*

a person should have kept on going.

17. *He drew back from the touch of*

a fist.

18. *The white girl who married the colored man*

was dopey.

19. *The most pleasant dreams*

are horrible.

20. *A drunken man*

should kill a person.

21. *No one can repair the damage caused by*

my fist.

22. *The nicest thing about being a child*

there isn't, don't write it.

23. *There is hardly any*

(examiner's name) left.

25. *Worse than being lonely is*

getting socked in the nose.

26. *When a person is ill*

he's sick I guess.

27. *A man can stop beating his wife only if*

he kisses her.

28. *The best thing about old age*

you don't have to work.

29. *Children are most annoying when*

they're not annoying — woops.

30. *If people only knew how much*

they liked (own full name) they'd be smart.

31. *The main difference between a wild and a tame animal is*

a wild animal comes up and purrs and a tame animal comes up and kills you.

32. *Few things are less attractive than*

none are less attractive than girls, no-no-take it back.

33. *The worst thing about being sick*

is that you can't run around.

34. *It is often hard to sleep when*

you have nightmares, no, when your little sister comes up and kisses you.

36. *To be a good liar one must*

tell the truth.

38. *People refrain from murder only because*

what's refrain from murder mean.

39. *Too much distance lies between*

me and—cross it out.

41. *There ought to be a law to*

be able to shoot BB guns.

42. *Spiders are*
>web makers.

43. *When a criminal leaves the prison he*
>becomes a criminal again probably, no, don't put probably.

44. *Compared with sisters brothers are*
>a lot better.

45. *The finger pointed*
>at the lion.

46. *Children are least annoying when*
>they're annoying—got to make it opposite.

47. *To avoid a fight one must*
>sock the other guy.

48. *A naked man*
>a woman would like to see.

49. *Closer and closer there comes*
>a snake.

50. *There would be more divorces*
>if—if—.

51. *A drunken woman*
>is smarter than a drunken man— no, I don't think so.

52. *When a person is wounded*
>he feels fine, I never think what I say.

53. *One's best friend may be irritating when*
>he starts punching you.

55. *A weak person does not often*
>keep from fighting.

56. *Down underground*
>worms and slugs and slimy things.

58. *Wouldn't it be really funny if*
>I saw somebody slip in a mud puddle.

59. *The kind of animal I would like most to be*

         is a human being — no, don't put that down—a horse or dog, half horse, half dog.

60. *Nothing is harder to stop than*

         (sister's name) mouth moving.

61. *The two most beautiful things I have ever seen*

         no, there aren't any.

64. *Failure may be expected when*

         a person sits down in an easy chair.

67. *The deeper one goes*

         the deeper.

68. *Behind one's back*

         I can do anything but in front of one's back I can't do anything.

71. *The worst kind of criminal*

         is the nicest man in the world.

73. *Tests like this*

         are stupid.

7. IRENE

Irene is a 25-year-old graduate student in psychology with very superior intelligence and creative ability.

1. *Children are usually certain that*

         they will have dinner.

2. *People are praised when*

         they do what is expected of them in an unexpected way.

3. *A large crowd*

         moves slowly.

4. *A person is most helpless when*

he doesn't understand what's going on.

5. *When an animal is wild*

it can use all its capacities, even though it suffers hardship in return for the privilege.

6. *The hardest decisions*

are the most interesting.

7. *The easiest way to get money*

is to work for it.

8. *Twenty years from now*

a great deal will have happened.

9. *Parents would worry less if*

they could feel less responsible for things beyond their control.

10. *When fire starts*

can smoke be far behind?

11. *Compared with dogs, cats are*

independent, and beautiful in movement rather than in structure.

12. *Fathers should learn that*

while they may control their wives by whining or by force, their children will depart, perhaps sooner in spirit than in body.

13. *One's closest friends can*

be closer than any kin.

14. *It is easy to get into trouble when*

you talk too much.

15. *Few children fear*

bloody knees.

16. *At the end of the road*
　　　　　　　　　　is a little house overlooking the ocean.

17. *He drew back from the touch of*
　　　　　　　　　　her hand.

18. *The white girl who married the colored man*
　　　　　　　　　　needed great strength to carry through the years ahead.

19. *The most pleasant dreams*
　　　　　　　　　　have more people than things in them.

20. *A drunken man*
　　　　　　　　　　is unpredictable, and usually boring.

21. *No one can repair the damage caused by*
　　　　　　　　　　unkind words.

22. *The nicest thing about being a child*
　　　　　　　　　　is not as nice as the rather ordinary things about being an adult.

23. *There is hardly any*
　　　　　　　　　　pet nicer than a cat.

24. *To be without shame*
　　　　　　　　　　is to be free.

25. *Worse than being lonely is*
　　　　　　　　　　hard to imagine.

26. *When a person is ill*
　　　　　　　　　　it is hard to talk to him naturally.

27. *A man can stop beating his wife only if*
　　　　　　　　　　he has verbal ability.

28. *The best thing about old age*
　　　　　　　　　　is having free time to enjoy what other people are doing.

29. *Children are most annoying when*
　　　　　　　　　　they are trying to be cute.

30. *If people only knew how much*

> I like some of them.

31. *The main difference between a wild and a tame animal is*

> that the wild animal is beautiful to look at, and the tame animal is nice to touch.

32. *Few things are less attractive than*

> "proper" women's clothing.

33. *The worst thing about being sick*

> is that you can't use the time you're taking off from work.

34. *It is often hard to sleep when*

> too many exciting things have happened.

35. *People shouldn't*

> jump to conclusions.

36. *To be a good liar one must*

> believe the lies oneself.

37. *A masculine woman should*

> be pitied.

38. *People refrain from murder only because*

> it's not very constructive.

39. *Too much distance lies between*

> New York and our summer cabin.

40. *The best of mothers may forget that*

> their daughters' lives are not theirs.

41. *There ought to be a law to*

> prevent monopolies effectively.

42. *Spiders are*

> horrid insects who make pretty webs.

43. *When a criminal leaves the prison he*

has a tremendous job ahead of him.

44. *Compared with sisters brothers are*

less intense.

45. *The finger pointed*

to the door.

46. *Children are least annoying when*

(this item not included in version administered).

47. *To avoid a fight one must*

be very clever.

48. *A naked man*

is beautiful and funny.

49. *Closer and closer there comes*

the end of the term.

50. *There would be more divorces if*

martyrs didn't do so well in our society.

51. *A drunken woman*

is unattractive.

52. *When a person is wounded*

he draws into himself.

53. *One's best friend may be irritating when*

one wants to try a new role.

54. *A woman's body*

can be beautiful or disgusting.

55. *A weak person does not often*

change much.

56. *Down underground*

there are pipes, wires, and subways.

57. *One can hardly see*

why some activities are considered interesting.

58. *Wouldn't it be really funny if*

bees were bears. (cf. Winnie-the-Pooh)

59. *The kind of animal I would like most to be*

is a soft, fuzzy, lady pussy-cat.

60. *Nothing is harder to stop than*

reading a good story.

61. *The two most beautiful things I have ever seen*

are the ocean and mountains with a little fog on top.

62. *She couldn't bear to touch*

the bubble and make it break even sooner.

63. *A woman who has lost her virtue must*

get along without it.

64. *Failure may be expected when*

other things distract a person, child, or customers from the business at hand.

65. *An effeminate man may*

have been a very nice boy.

66. *It hurts when*

the dentist drills.

67. *The deeper one goes*

the more fascinating it is.

68. *Behind one's back*

one sees nothing.

69. *When the car skidded*

I was scared to death.

70. *A mother is more likely than a father to*

work her hands "to the bone" for her children.

71. *The worst kind of criminal*

is a blackmailer.

72. *If one cannot own*

> one must rent.

73. *Tests like this*

> are difficult if one tries
> to be neither superficial
> nor artificial.

A central feature of Irene's personality as revealed in her sentence completion is her persistent underestimation, sometimes with awareness and sometimes not, of her own capabilities. This underestimation is accompanied by sensitivity and perceptiveness toward people and events which provide her with ample cognitive evidence of her ability. It would appear that this pattern of response was determined to a considerable degree in her childhood by demands for conformity to adult standards, an essentially weak father and a mother who perhaps overcompensated for paternal deficiencies.

"12. Fathers should learn that / while they may control their wives by whining or by force, their children will depart, perhaps sooner in spirit than in body.

50. There would be more divorces if / martyrs didn't do so well in our society.

70. A mother is more likely than a father to / work her hands "to the bone" for her children.

40. The best of mothers may forget that / their daughters' lives are not theirs.

41. There ought to be a law to / prevent monopolies effectively.

22. The nicest thing about being a child / is not as nice as the rather ordinary things about being an adult."

She doesn't trust herself to act without inhibition, although there is no evidence that to do so would be unsafe. She alternates between the appearance of stubbornness on the one hand and docility on the other, both attitudes derived from an exaggerated sense of her own weakness.   With alternating successes and self-doubts ("62. She couldn't bear to touch / the bubble and make it break even sooner)," she has no stable mood, but goes back and forth between mild elation and moderate depression. The more mastery she achieves over external affairs, the less certain she is that she deserves it, and the more concerned she gets about her own role. In moments of self-doubt she may temporarily, but only temporarily, fall back on an attitude of conformity with authority, but she recovers quickly and comes to grips with the actual issues involved.

"13. One's closest friends can / be closer than any kin.

30. If people only knew how much / I liked some of them.

53. One's best friend may be irritating when / one wants to try a new role.

19. The most pleasant dreams / have more people than things in them."

The intensity of her response, the nature of her recurring conflicts, and her ability to make creative use of both the conflicts and her insight into them, are reflected in the following responses:

"44. Compared with sisters brothers are / less intense.

5. When an animal is wild / it can use all its capacities, even though it suffers hardship in return for the privilege.

42. Spiders are / horrid insects who make pretty webs.

53. One's best friend may be irritating when / one wants to try a new role.

6. The hardest decisions / are the most interesting.

67. The deeper one goes / the more fascinating it is.

2. People are praised when / they do what is expected of them in an unexpected way."

8. JEREMY

Jeremy is a well adjusted 43-year-old man of superior intelligence engaged in technical management work in the administrative service of a large corporation.

1. Children are usually certain that

their parents enjoy more privileges than they do.

2. People are praised when

they deserve it or when it suits the purpose of the praise giver.

3. A large crowd

provides anonymity for the individual.

4. A person is most helpless when

he is controlled by adverse circumstances.

5. When an animal is wild

he does not know it.

6. The hardest decisions

are those which impinge on the rights or desires of others.

7. The easiest way to get money

is to persuade people they need something you can provide.

8. *Twenty years from now*

the changes will exceed the changes of the preceding 40 years.

9. *Parents would worry less if*

someone else shared their responsibilities.

10. *When fire starts*

quick calculations are required as to the means of minimizing the damage.

11. *Compared with dogs, cats are*

more introverted.

12. *Fathers should learn that*

children teach.

13. *One's closest friends can*

provide most comfort and irritation.

14. *It is easy to get into trouble when*

impulse dominates conduct.

15. *Few children fear*

bearers of gifts.

16. *At the end of the road*

is the uncertainty of adventure.

17. *He drew back from the touch of*

the strange animal.

18. *The white girl who married the colored man*

was handicapped by the distrust of her neighbors.

19. *The most pleasant dreams*

are those that seem attainable in reality.

20. *A drunken man*

pursues a dream.

21. *No one can repair the damage caused by*

persistent hatred.

22. *The nicest thing about being a child*

is the anticipation of glory.

23. *There is hardly any*

point at which to begin this completion.

24. *To be without shame*

is like being without eyes.

25. *Worse than being lonely is*

not being able to enjoy your own company.

26. *When a person is ill*

he can enjoy the help of others.

27. *A man can stop beating his wife only if*

it hurts her more than it hurts him.

28. *The best thing about old age*

is the enjoyment of free speech without responsibility.

29. *Children are most annoying when*

they exercise their prerogative of being irresponsible.

30. *If people only knew how much*

of life is trial and error.

31. *The main difference between a wild and a tame animal is*
fear of man.

32. *Few things are less attractive than*

an image of a personal fault as reflected by another.

33. *The worst thing about being sick*

is the unpredictability of the course and the length of the disorder.

34. *It is often hard to sleep when*

a great expectation has been threatened.

35. *People shouldn't*

          jump at conclusions.

36. *To be a good liar one must*

          have confidence in the lie.

37. *A masculine woman should*

          cultivate both sexes.

38. *People refrain from murder only because*

          you can't get away with it.

39. *Too much distance lies between*

          the minds that try to meet.

40. *The best of mothers may forget that*

          childhood is a pathway to independence.

41. *There ought to be a law to*

          increase the highway capacity in proportion to the number of new cars.

42. *Spiders are*

          spinners and weavers.

43. *When a criminal leaves the prison he*

          hopes he won't come back.

44. *Compared with sisters brothers are*

          more useful in a fight.

45. *The finger pointed*

          toward the heavens.

46. *Children are least annoying when*

          asleep.

47. *To avoid a fight one must*

          avoid the obvious forms of self-assertion.

48. *A naked man*

          is not likely to make a public appearance.

49. *Closer and closer there comes*

          the end of the ferry ride.

50. *There would be more divorces if*

          finding a new spouse were not such a bother.

51. *A drunken woman*

  may need protection.

52. *When a person is wounded*

  he should be helped.

53. *One's best friend may be irritating when*

  he indicates awareness of one's shortcomings.

54. *A woman's body*

  is one of the seven wonders.

55. *A weak person does not often*

  inspire confidence.

56. *Down underground*

  is the past and the un-known.

57. *One can hardly see*

  the blades of a spinning propeller.

58. *Wouldn't it be really funny if*

  the examiner could make nothing of this.

59. *The kind of animal I would like most to be*

  is a phoenix.

60. *Nothing is harder to stop than*

  the leak at the bottom of the boat.

61. *The two most beautiful things I have ever seen*

  will have to be re-created out of my memory in some more poetic mood.

62. *She couldn't bear to touch*

  the thing that had hurt her.

64. *Failure may be expected when*

  the goals are set too high.

65. *An effeminate man may*

  have difficulty in finding fulfillment.

66. *It hurts when*
> the doctor jabs his needle in.

67. *The deeper one goes*
> the more one finds.

68. *Behind one's back*
> one's friends can be more relaxed.

69. *When the car skidded*
> the heart went to the throat.

70. *A mother is more likely than a father*
> to attribute glamor to motherhood.

71. *The worst kind of criminal*
> is the kind that doesn't get caught.

72. *If one cannot own*
> one can depreciate ownership.

73. *Tests like this*
> scare the wary and spare the scary.

This sentence completion reflects a mature appraisal of authority, both with respect to his acceptance of it when he is in a subordinate role and his appreciation of his own responsibility when he is in a dominant role.

"15. Few children fear / bearers of gifts.
16. The nicest thing about being a child / is the anticipation of glory.
12. Fathers should learn that / children teach.
28. The best thing about old age / is the enjoyment of free speech without responsibility."

Jeremy needs and wants the support and company of people and is willing to go more than half way.

"13. One's closest friends can / provide most comfort. . . .

26. When a person is ill / he can enjoy the help of others.

27. A man can stop beating his wife only if / it hurts her more than it hurts him.

39. Too much distance lies between / the minds that try to meet."

But even so, he is in many respects a lonely person.

"13. One's closest friends can / provide most. . . . irritation.

32. Few things are less attractive than / an image of a personal fault as reflected by another.

68. Behinds one's back / one's friends can be more relaxed.

25. Worse than being lonely is / not being able to enjoy your own company.

3. A large crowd / provides anonymity for the individual."

It is clear that Jeremy is keenly aware of complexity both outside and within himself and that his responses to it are highly philosophical and contemplative. Without denying the existence of issues he avoids personal challenge presented by others and offers little himself.

There is a large measure of self-abnegation in his responses. This property which might easily be a liability seems rather to have been converted into an asset by sustaining a high value on broad and tolerant social utility.

One can only speculate on the response to 59. "The kind of animal I would like most to be / is a phoenix." There are many legends about this eagle-like bird with red

and golden plumage which perpetuated itself in an endless cycle of destruction and rebirth. For Herodotus the
phoenix bore his father embalmed in myrrh for burial in
the temple of the sun. For Pliny the phoenix built himself
a nest of cassia and frankincense upon which he was about
to die. For Tacitus the phoenix burned his father on the
altar of the sun. For Horappolo the phoenix supplied
from self-inflicted wounds the juices from which the young
phoenix springs. But all authorities agree on one point.
There is only one contemporary phoenix.

9. KENMORE

Kenmore is 34 years old, an inadequate personality who
is unable in his weakness and dependence to manage his
life or even to hold a job. He uses his disease, diabetes,
as a way of increasing and justifying his dependence.

1. *Children are usually certain that*

    they'll miss the bus if
    they're not standing on the
    corner in time.

2. *People are praised when*

    they do a good deed.

3. *A large crowd*

    gathered for the conven-
    tion.

4. *A person is most helpless when*

    he's sick.

5. *When an animal is wild*

    he's usually confined to a
    cage.

6. *The hardest decisions*

    are usually the best.

7. *The easiest way to get money*

    to steal it.

8. *Twenty years from now*

    I won't be here.

9. *Parents would worry less if*

their children would do better.

10. *When fire starts*

there's a warmth.

11. *Compared with dogs, cats are*

the same family.

12. *Fathers should learn that*

obedience from the children is very helpful.

13. *One's closest friends can*

sometimes deceive him.

14. *It is easy to get into trouble when*

you're brought up wrong. or don't have any parents in your young days.

15. *Few children fear*

their parents.

16. *At the end of the road*

there is usually a turning.

17. *He drew back from the touch of*

the other person.

18. *The white girl who married the colored man*

unbeknown to her parents, was told never to come home again.

19. *The most pleasant dreams*

usually bring such old memories.

20. *A drunken man*

is usually broke.

21. *No one can repair the damage caused by*

injuring the hip bone.

22. *The nicest thing about being a child*

you don't have to pay the bills.

23. *There is hardly any*

milk left in the can—I'll have to make these simpler.

24. *To be without shame*

is as bad as being without your good suit on Sunday.

25. *Worse than being lonely is*

solitary confinement.

26. *When a person is ill*

he seems to have more worries.

27. *A man can stop beating his wife only if*

his conscience tells him to.

28. *The best thing about old age*

old age pension.

29. *Children are most annoying when*

company arrives.

30. *If people only knew how much*

their parents loved them they would do better.

31. *The main difference between a wild and a tame animal is*

in their actions.

32. *Few things are less attractive than*

moss on a hill side.

33. *The worst thing about being sick*

you don't feel much like participating in athletic games.

34. *It is often hard to sleep when*

you drink coffee at night.

35. *People shouldn't*

talk back to parents.

36. *To be a good liar one must*

stick to it I guess.

37. *A masculine woman should*

I don't understand that.

38. People refrain from murder only because
> they know better.

39. Too much distance lies between
> our foreign nations.

40. The best of mothers may forget that
> their children's ages.
> That's about the only thing
> I know a mother would
> forget—It wouldn't be the
> love for them.

41. There ought to be a law to

> barring drunks from driv-
> ing cars.

42. Spiders are

> usually dangerous.

43. When a criminal leaves the prison he

> usually goes on the right
> track.

44. Compared with sisters brothers are

> the stronger sex.

45. The finger pointed

> toward the guilty party.

46. Children are least annoying when

> (not included in version
> administered).

47. To avoid a fight one must

> control his temper.

48. A naked man

49. Closer and closer there comes

> conflict between the ar-
> mies.

50. There would be more divorces if

> you didn't have to pay to
> get them.

51. A drunken woman

> shakes—is a worse sort of
> looking person than a man
> when they're drunk.

52. *When a person is wounded*

he needs medical care.

53. *One's best friend may be irritating when*

you're among them.

54. *A woman's body*

is made up of quite a few different parts.

55. *A weak person does not often*

go ahead in all stages of life—he's backward.

56. *Down underground*

the subway trains can be heard.

57. *One can hardly see*

with his eyes partly closed.

58. *Wouldn't it be really funny if*

Romeo and Juliet were two real characters.

59. *The kind of animal I would like most to be*

an ape.

60. *Nothing is harder to stop than*

a moving object.

61. *The two most beautiful things I have ever seen*

well, the Endless Caverns and Stone Mountain in Georgia.

62. *She couldn't bear to touch*

his hand.

63. *A woman who has lost her virtue must*

change her walk of life.

64. *Failure may be expected when*

one doesn't keep good book accounts.

65. *An effeminate man may*

don't know what that means.

66. *It hurts when*

you cut your hand.

67. *The deeper one goes*

in the mine the more coal he'll get.

68. *Behind one's back*

people often talk about you.

69. *When the car skidded*

it struck the tree.

70. *A mother is more likely than a father to*

caress her child.

71. *The worst kind of criminal*

is usually hardened.

72. *If one cannot own*

an automobile he has to seek other means of transportation.

73. *Tests like this*

are very educational—I don't know what it has to do with my sickness.

With great frequency, analysis of sentence completion material leads to the formulation of personality description in terms of important conflicts within the subject. Kenmore's personality lends itself easily to portrayal in terms of contrasts and apparent paradoxes, but the infantility, the dependence, the refusal—indeed, the inability—to assume responsibility, make him too weak a person to be described as sustaining conflicts. He is flexible but not resilient, docile but not helpful, relaxed but not comfortable, suspicious but not paranoid. He is ambitious but without goals, pushed rapidly but not going anywhere, pessimistic without having any disaster in mind. He is petty but without real attention to detail, has concern for order but is unable to distinguish between order and disorder. He has poor impulse control but few impulses, he is emotionally stable but has little emotion.

If others will take the responsibility, he will hope for the best, but he doesn't expect too much—he knows he is pretty weak. No doubt he feels that if he were not sick, things would be different, but he is sick, so he doesn't have to risk finding out.

10. LUKE

Luke is a 30-year-old hospitalized paranoid schizophrenic.

1. Children are usually certain that

what you think.

2. People are praised when

they are talkative or something.

3. A large crowd

demonstration.

4. A person is most helpless when

he meets someone he knows, I guess.

5. When an animal is wild

it's dangerous.

6. The hardest decisions

well, if you'd be in charge of some men or something important that you have in command.

7. The easiest way to get money

is to have a monopoly or to work for it.

8. Twenty years from now

what should happen? Oh, wouldn't be much different—just same machine.

9. Parents would worry less if

I had friends, good friends.

10. *When fire starts*

if you don't have equipment to put it out, just run for your life.

11. *Compared with dogs, cats are*

that would be more like a jungle, wouldn't it?

12. *Fathers should learn that*

take care of his children.

13. *One's closest friends can*

oh well, many things—hard to say—probably do anything.

14. *It is easy to get into trouble when*

you're intoxicated or making a scene.

15. *Few children fear*

you know, from evil—from being scared.

16. *At the end of the road*

stop, I guess.

17. *He drew back from the touch of*

iron.

18. *The white girl who married the colored man*

well, she must be crazy.

19. *The most pleasant dreams*

well, getting married I guess.

20. *A drunken man*

well it's hard to say—I never used to get drunk— oh I don't know—they lay on the floor, the ground.

21. *No one can repair the damage caused by*

machine.

22. *The nicest thing about being a child*

is to meet other children.

23. *There is hardly any*

    friendship like it's supposed to be.

24. *To be without shame*

    is to have and to hold, I guess.

25. *Worse than being lonely is*

    having people interfere with something you're about to do.

26. *When a person is ill*

    there's not much you can do to try and help him.

27. *A man can stop beating his wife only if*

    he'd get about and be talkative.

28. *The best thing about old age*

    well sit and talk—well, somebody would probably take care of you.

29. *Children are most annoying when*

    they're not seen—at school or something.

30. *If people only knew how much*

    it would depend on what kind of people—if you had your own you'd be naturally talkative.

31. *The main difference between a wild and a tame animal is*

    the wild would probably be—well, more respectful, sit and talk (Q) the tame one probably—the wild is a walker.

32. *Few things are less attractive than*

    people.

33. *The worst thing about being sick*

    well, it would probably be miscrable.

34. It is often hard to sleep when

you haven't got, you know, couldn't get along with somebody—for instance a girl you'd known.

35. People shouldn't

show what kind of—be where they're not supposed to.

36. To be a good liar one must

probably be a gambler.

37. A masculine woman should

it depends what she had in mind.

38. People refrain from murder only because

somebody—they must have been known by their own people—they must have been in—probably be an attempt or something.

39. Too much distance lies between

me and you.

40. The best of mothers may forget that

there was a machine or something—a deadly weapon they're making—that's what killed them.

41. There ought to be a law to

you know, to watch these here—quitting I guess. There's not much you could do with a policeman.

42. Spiders are

insects that more or less— that a man that takes an interest in insect life— probably be deadly scared of them.

43. *When a criminal leaves the prison he*

> I don't believe there was any criminals at all at one time.

44. *Compared with sisters brothers are*

> more policeman and more of a —

45. *The finger pointed*

> that would be—you would have run an errand.

46. *Children are least annoying when*

> you keep them.

47. *To avoid a fight one must*

> well it's not to carry any harmful tools.

48. *A naked man*

> well, he'd probably be a swimmer.

49. *Closer and closer there comes*

> what? well it would probably be, you know, friendship or something.

50. *There would be more divorces if*

> well it would depend what you had in mind—if you intend to marry forever or just for a while.

51. *A drunken woman*

> I never seen any—like today.

52. *When a person is wounded*

> by what? by an arm? he'd probably be taken care of if he were known.

53. *One's best friend may be irritating when*

> he has an arm that ain't supposed to be—I mean like a horrible arm or something—like a color.

54. A woman's body

well it's more sanction, sacrilegous of life.

55. A weak person does not often

say anything.

56. Down underground

is a cemetery.

57. One can hardly see

when something is—somebody you know—something wrong — somebody you know to be respectable.

58. Wouldn't it be really funny if

the world came to an end.

59. The kind of animal I would like most to be

well, it's difficult. You would probably want the skin—you know—want the skin for a coat or something.

60. Nothing is harder to stop than

yourself, I guess.

61. The two most beautiful things I have ever seen

would probably be people.

62. She couldn't bear to touch

depending on what was going on at the present.

63. A woman who has lost her virtue must

be insane, I guess.

64. Failure may be expected when

everybody had success once, didn't they?

65. An effeminate man may

probably be a good sailor or soldier.

66. It hurts when

you had something and you lost.

67. *The deeper one goes*

well, it wouldn't be deeper —it would probably be a boat.

68. *Behind one's back*

they were all trusted.

69. *When the car skidded*

it probably cracked up.

70. *A mother is more likely than a father to*

me.

71. *The worst kind of criminal*

is a man who has a sense-less tool which he could have took out murdering.

72. *If one cannot own*

property—if you can't own you must have had it—generation you know where they had been living.

73. *Tests like this*

is a—well it uh—doesn't do me much good but probably helps you.

If one judges by conventional standards, Luke is clearly deteriorated. Furthermore, in the light of his coherence in the recent past he might be said to be rapidly deteriorating. He talks repetitiously about the "machine," and his feeling that talkativeness is important stands out in his record.

This sentence completion, however, does not leave us with the feeling of frustrated effort at understanding which is so common in dealing conversationally with paranoid schizophrenics.

Throughout the record Luke seems to be trying desperately to make contact with people. Children are certain that / what you think. People are praised when / they are talkative.

He does not succeed. The inexorable machine-like qualities of adjustment are imposed upon him, personally. And life becomes a machine. One draws back from the touch of iron. But the damage by the machine continues.

Only children are free. They meet other children—not machines.

In this record one can, without too much effort, make a beginning at communication with a paranoid schizophrenic.

11. MELVIN

Melvin, age thirty, found the sentences difficult to complete and suggested that he be given permission to change the openings. Permission was given and the results, with his changes indicated by parentheses, demonstrate how little essential difference such changes may make despite the strong need to make them. (Deletions from the openings are indicated by italic type in parentheses; additions to the openings are indicated by roman type in parentheses.)

At the time of this examination there was some uncertainty about the nature of Melvin's psychological problem—and by no means complete agreement as to whether he had any problem at all of psychological importance. He was affable, friendly, and somewhat reserved. He appeared to be a little pompous and condescending but no more so than could be tolerated by most of his associates. Although our primary purpose in the inclusion of the record is to illustrate how unsuccessful the effort to evade by changing the opening may be, there is the additional value of showing how a record may point convincingly toward the existence of systematized pathology. Note 1, 3, 4, 13, 14, 22, 29, 32, 34, 47, and the large number and the nature of the openings to which he was unable to respond despite the unlimited latitude he was permitted in changing them.

1. *Children are usually certain that*
      Life is just one big game.

2. *People are* (generally) *praised when*
      They have done something exceptional.

3. (When I am in) *a large crowd*
      Such as a department store, I am quite uncomfortable.

4. *A person is most helpless when*
      He is sick and cannot control himself.

5. (*When an animal is wild*)
      A wild animal is much more adjusted than an animal taken into captivity.

6. (*The hardest decisions*)
      Some of the easiest situations sometimes present *the hardest decisions.*

7. (No doubt) *the easiest way to get money*
      Is to earn it.

8. (It is impossible to predict what situations and events will take place.)
      twenty years from now.

9. (*Parents would worry less if*)
      The more parents understand their children the less they worry.

10. When (a) *fire starts*
      It spreads rapidly.

11. (*Compared with dogs, cats are*)

> In so far as pets are concerned dogs are much better than cats.

12. (*Fathers should learn that*)

> When a man becomes a father he must learn that he has greatly increased his responsibility.

13. (It is always well to discuss matters with)

> *One's closest friends* (*can*) but at the same time *one's closest friends can* turn out to be one's worst enemies.

14. (If a person lacks self control and confidence)

> *It is easy to get into trouble* (*when*).

15. *Few children fear*

> Growing up or fear the future.

16. (*At the end of the road*)

> Very few roads end.

17. *He drew back from the touch of*

18. (When a) (*The*) *white girl* (*who*) *marrie*(*d*)*s* (*the*) (*a*) *colored man*

> She can expect many difficulties and much unhappiness.

19. (*The most*) *pleasant dreams*

> Rarely come true and sometimes influence a person's aims.

20. *A drunken man*

> Can many times not be criticized for his action.

21. (*No one can repair the*) *damage caused by*

Words spoken in the heat of passion cannot be repaired.

22. (One of) *the nicest thing*(s) *about* (*being a*) *child*

Hood is the lack of knowledge of the true happenings in every day life.

23. *There is hardly any*

24. *To be without shame*

Is to be without humor—Proverb.

25. (*Worse than being lonely is*)

One of the worst things existing is being lonely.

26. (*When*) *a person is* (*ill*)

Often extremely helpless when he is ill.

27. *A man can stop beating his wife only if*

28. (*The best thing about old age*)

At a young age most people can see very few good things about old age.

29. (*Children are most annoying when*)

When children are underdisciplined and uncontrollable they can be extremely annoying.

30. (*If people only knew how much*)

Very few people realize how little they actually know.

31. (*The main difference between a wild and tame animal is*)

A wild animal is much happier in his wild state than a tame animal which tends to lose his natural instincts.

32. *Few things are less attractive than*

> Can't exactly say—take a lot of thought.

33. *The worst thing about being sick*

> Is that a person can do little to help himself.

34. (*It is often hard to sleep when*)

> Worry or deep concentration about one or many subjects sometimes make it difficult to sleep.

35. (Some) *people shouldn't*

> Be so quick to criticize others.

36. *To be a good liar one must*

37. *A masculine woman should*

> Seek work and recreation to fit her personality.

38. (Most) *people refrain from murder* (*only*) *because*

> It is contrary to what they are taught and in some cases it is due to fear of the law.

39. (Sometimes there is not) *too much distance* (*lies*) *between*

> Good and bad, truth and fiction.

40. *The best of mothers may forget that*

> They are also wives—doubt.

41. *There ought to be a law to*

42. *Spiders are*

43. (*When a criminal leaves the prison he*)

> It is often difficult for a man to readjust himself or for others to realize his problems when he leaves prison.

44. *Compared with sisters brothers are*

45. *The finger pointed*

46. (*Children are least annoying when*)

> When children are well brought up and are contented they are generally least annoying.

47. (If a person chooses) *To avoid a fight* (*one must*)

> He must exercise self control and be reasonable.

48. *A naked man*

> Can't answer.

49. *Closer and closer there comes*

> Only in fiction.

50. *There would be more divorces if*

> The divorce laws were less strict.

51. *A drunken woman*

> Hard to answer.

52. *When a person is wounded*

> He must not become excited or panicky.

53. *One's best friend may be irritating when*

> He takes your friendship too much for granted and not understand your moods.

54. *A woman's body*

> Can be a thing of great beauty.

55. *A* (physically) *weak person does not often*

> Excel in athletics and a mentally weak person does not often succeed in life.

56. *Down underground*

> Lie many great resources beneficial to civilization.

57. *One can hardly see*

> Many benefits arriving from supposedly great decisions.

58. *Wouldn't it be really funny if*

59. *The kind of animal I would like most to be*

60. *Nothing is harder to stop than*

61. *The two most beautiful things I have ever seen*

62. *She couldn't bear to touch*

63. (The idea of a) *A woman who has lost her virtue (must)*

> In most cases is not so serious.

64. *Failure may be expected when*

> Effort is lacking.

65. *An effeminate man (may)*

> Should seek for a cure.

66. *It hurts when*

67. *The deeper one goes*

> The more he learns.

68. (Things that go on) *Behind one's back*

> Are not always important and can be disregarded but also can be damaging.

69. *When the car skidded*

> He lost control.

70. *A mother is more likely than a father to*

> Be lenient—children.

71. *The worst kind of criminal*

> Is a dope peddler.

72. *If one cannot own*

73. *Tests like this*

12. NATHAN

Nathan is a late adolescent juvenile delinquent. He has a long history of misbehavior and arrests. The court finally determined that something more than and different from probation would be required to alter his behavior.

This is the record of a young man who feels the need to battle for what he gets but is really too timid to initiate the fight. He wants adult prerogatives but is unwilling to assume adult responsibility. He gives quick, self-protective lip service to conventional ethical and moral precepts, but without real concern about abiding by them. He is dependent on external controls with a minimum of internal ones.

Note particularly 3, 6, 7, 8, 14, 19, 22, 24, 28, 33, 34, 36, 43, 47, 48, 51, 54, 55, 58, 64, 66, 70.

1. *Children are usually certain that*

   they are right.

2. *People are praised when*

   they do something good.

3. *A large crowd*

   means trouble.

4. *A person is most helpless when*

   he is alone.

5. *When an animal is wild*

   he is savage.

6. *The hardest decisions*

   are worrisome.

7. *The easiest way to get money*

   is to find it.

8. *Twenty years from now*

   I will be working.

9. *Parents would worry less if*

   your home.

10. *When fire starts*

call the fire dept.

11. *Compared with dogs, cats are*

frail.

12. *Fathers should learn that*

——

13. *One's closest friends can*

help him.

14. *It is easy to get into trouble when*

you need money.

15. *Few children fear*

dogs.

16. *At the end of the road*

you stop.

17. *He drew back from the touch of*

the man.

18. *The white girl who married the colored man*

must love him.

19. *The most pleasant dreams*

are the sweetest ones.

20. *A drunken man*

doesn't know what he is doing.

21. *No one can repair the damage caused by*

fire.

22. *The nicest thing about being a child*

is having plenty of time to play.

23. *There is hardly any*

——

24. *To be without shame*

is disgraceful.

25. *Worse than being lonely is*

being dead.

26. *When a person is ill*
   > he is sick.

27. *A man can stop beating his wife only if*
   > she stops him.

28. *The best thing about old age*
   > is social security.

29. *Children are most annoying when*
   > they make noise.

30. *If people only knew how much*
   > you cared.

31. *The main difference between a wild and a tame animal is*
   > one is domesticated and
   > the other is savage.

32. *Few things are less attractive than*
   > others.

33. *The worst thing about being sick*
   > is when it hurts.

34. *It is often hard to sleep when*
   > you worry.

35. *People shouldn't*
   > steal.

36. *To be a good liar one must*
   > have a straight face.

37. *A masculine woman should*
   > wrestle.

38. *People refrain from murder only because*
   > they want to.

39. *Too much distance lies between*
   > some peoples mouths.

40. *The best of mothers may forget that*
   > ——

41. *There ought to be a law to*
   > ——

42. *Spiders are*
   > gruesome.

43. *When a criminal leaves the prison he*

is happy.

44. *Compared with sisters brothers are*

not so good looking.

45. *The finger pointed*

thataway.

46. *Children are least annoying when*

they are sleeping.

47. *To avoid a fight one must*

run.

48. *A naked man*

should dress.

49. *Closer and closer there comes*

——

50. *There would be more divorces if*

there were more mar-
riages.

51. *A drunken woman*

is disgraceful.

52. *When a person is wounded*

he should call for help.

53. *One's best friend may be irritating when*

he tells the truth.

54. *A woman's body*

is fragile compared to
man.

55. *A weak person does not often*

fight.

56. *Down underground*

is dirt.

57. *One can hardly see*

in a blizzard.

58. *Wouldn't it be really funny if*

I had a car.

59. *The kind of animal I would like most to be*

——

60. *Nothing is harder to stop than*
     a wild elephant.
61. *The two most beautiful things I have ever seen*
     were Niagara Falls.
62. *She couldn't bear to touch*
     him.
63. *A woman who has lost her virtue must*
     ——
64. *Failure may be expected when*
     you dont try.
65. *An effeminate man may*
     do crazy things.
65. *It hurts when*
     you get hit.
67. *The deeper one goes*
     deeper.
68. *Behind one's back*
     is something he can't see.
69. *When the car skidded*
     it crashed.
70. *A mother is more likely than a father to*
     cry.
71. *The worst kind of criminal*
     is a murderer.
72. *If one cannot own*
     ——
73. *Tests like this*
     make you think.

13. OPHELIA

Ophelia, age 50, consulted a physician about vague but distressing somatic symptoms. The physician, suspecting an important psychic component in her complaint, referred her for psychological diagnostic study. Ten days later she committed suicide by taking an overdose of barbiturate.

1. Children are usually certain that

father and mother aren't far away (laughs).

2. People are praised when

they are successful.

3. A large crowd

is not something that I care about (laughs).

4. A person is most helpless when

well, incapacitated in any way. I shouldn't say that, I should say . . . .

5. When an animal is wild

oh, dear, I cant think what to say about that, I (laughs) think they are more frightened than anything else, or vicious.

6. The hardest decisions

all decisions are hard.

7. The easiest way to get money

that I wouldn't know; there's no easy way.

8. Twenty years from now

I hope the world will have made progress.

9. Parents would worry less if

(pause) if they paid more time and attention to their children; perhaps I wouldn't know, that is a hard one, you can say so much about that.

10. When fire starts

is that the first, "When fire starts?"—it's either a great blessing or a great horror.

11. *Compared with dogs, cats are*

in a class by themselves (laugh).

12. *Fathers should learn that*

you can't do everything all at once.

13. *One's closest friends can*

one doesn't always know one's closest friends.

14. *It is easy to get into trouble when*

one isn't careful.

15. *Few children fear*

oh, could say a lot about that—love.

16. *At the end of the road*

turn right (laugh).

17. *He drew back from the touch of*

her hand (laugh).

18. *The white girl who married the colored man*

(not given).

19. *The most pleasant dreams*

are wishful thinking.

20. *A drunken man*

is a pest.

21. *No one can repair the damage caused by*

misunderstanding, that isn't quite true; no, that isn't true; fatal accidents, I guess.

22. *The nicest thing about being a child*

is not being grown up (laugh).

23. *There is hardly any*

(pause) well, the only thing. . .there is hardly any problem that can't be solved by the right thinking and attention and care.

24. *To be without shame*

is not a human quality.

25. *Worse than being lonely is*

oh, there are an awful lot of things, to be an object of charity, I guess.

26. *When a person is ill*

worries and cares multiply.

27. *A man can stop beating his wife only if*

he starts (laugh).

28. *The best thing about old age*

is to have lived a good life.

29. *Children are most annoying when*

they don't understand.

30. *If people only knew how much*

they could accomplish if they set their minds to it.

31. *The main difference between a wild and a tame animal is*

I wouldn't know, I can't express that; I suppose you could say accident of birth and surroundings.

32. *Few things are less attractive than*

pitiful personalities.

33. *The worst thing about being sick*

(pause) I guess you say the trouble and effect you might have on those surrounding you.

34. *It is often hard to sleep when*

it is either too loud or too quiet. And when you are not sleepy is really the answer to that; that is the answer to that.

35. *People shouldn't*

think too much about themselves.

36. *To be a good liar one must*

be clever.

37. *A masculine woman should*

> oh, heavens, what a question; not that really; should probably raise horses (laugh).

38. *People refrain from murder only because*

> well, that is not a good question because you assume there that the people have murderous instincts and because their souls won't let them do it, I guess you may say.

39. *Too much distance lies between*

> what one can and what one would like to do; there are a lot of answers could be given to that one.

40. *The best of mothers may forget that*

> their children are human.

41. *There ought to be a law to*

> that is a catch phrase that should never be uttered.

42. *Spiders are*

> dreadful things (laugh) that's silly.

43. *When a criminal leaves the prison he*

> hopes he will never return.

44. *Compared with sisters brothers are*

> can't answer that question.

45. *The finger pointed*

> (pause) how can you deal with that question; I can't answer that question.

46. *Children are least annoying when*

> didn't you ask me that before? When they are quiet.

47. *To avoid a fight one must*

> control one's emotions.

48. A naked man

should be in bed (laugh)
shouldn't be naked
(laugh).

49. Closer and closer there comes

the marching on of time.

50. There would be more divorces if

most people were not,
well, I mean had religious
principles.

51. A drunken woman

is a pathetic thing.

52. When a person is wounded

they need help; that is not
right. . .he needs help.

53. One's best friend may be irritating when

he doesn't agree with you.

54. A woman's body

should be beautiful.

55. A weak person does not often

oh, that depends on the
person (pause) get into
as much trouble as a
strong one (laugh).

56. Down underground

can be traced the history
of the world.

57. One can hardly see

why one has to answer all
these questions.

58. Wouldn't it be really funny if

the unexpected always
happened.

59. The kind of animal I would like most to be

must I answer that literal-
ly? One that would be well
taken care of by humans.

60. Nothing is harder to stop than

a heated argument.

61. *The two most beautiful things I have ever seen*
>oh heavens, what a question, that is literal, too: I guess sunsets and mountain top.

62. *She couldn't bear to touch*
>the feather, I am thinking of housecleaning, I guess.

63. *A woman who has lost her virtue must*
>(pause) forget it (laugh).

64. *Failure may be expected when*
>an attempt is not made.

65. *An effeminate man may*
>overcome it.

66. *It hurts when*
>your best effort is thought nothing of.

67. *The deeper one goes*
>into things the more he will get out of them.

68. *Behind one's back*
>anything can happen.

69. *When the car skidded*
>luck alone will save you.

70. *A mother is more likely than a father to*
>be soft hearted in punishment— I am not sure about that; that is not the right answer; what was the question, "A woman" ... oh heavens...to provide the meals, I think that is true.

71. *The worst kind of criminal*
>is the intentional criminal.

72. *If one cannot own*

> I can't possibly—material
> wealth, he can still...he
> may perhaps be richer in
> spirit.

73. *Tests like this*

> seem somewhat superficial.

This record reveals a person who has high ambitions—but no goals; a strong need to succeed, but no ability to try; great dependence needs—but the inability to accept any support from others.

There is a great sense of helplessness accompanied by disorganization in her thinking. She feels weak, perplexed, confused, with a lost and hopeless orientation toward people, and a loss of systematized interests or plans. On the surface she is tense, but at a deeper level there is flatness and emptiness. She lives in a world which she feels entirely powerless to modify. She lacks standards, goals, any sense of her own identity as an individual, but feels nevertheless hemmed in by prohibitions and by the certainty of failure. The picture of a woman convinced of her own worthlessness, confused, and at the edge of panic, offers some clarification of the subsequent self-destruction.

Chapter VI

POSTSCRIPT

THE FOLLOWING GOALS now seem to us reasonable and desirable. They have determined the direction and amount of our own effort, and we hope we have provided a constructive stimulus to the reader so that he can approach them more closely.

Psychologists who are increasingly turning toward the application of their knowledge and skills to the solution of personal adjustment problems, and physicians who deal with mental illness are in great need of more effective, practicable, economical and meaningful instruments for clinical diagnosis. The staggering number of persons who need help, and the absolute impossibility of training in the predictable future the number of professional personnel required to deal with them, forbid our spending two hours on a job which conceivably may be done in one. Nor can we waste time in the use of examining techniques which *may* throw light on a problem if we can develop a method which quite probably will.

Social and experimental psychologists are in need of techniques of approach to areas of psychological importance such as affect, emotion, character, and personality, These areas have long been especially resistant to objective attack. Accumulation of convincing evidence has required the expenditure of many hours of interpersonal contact, often with the disappointing result that communication is difficult and comparison of findings of different observers impossible because the basic data are not available.

(171)

Two major trends of psychological progress in the last half century have been clear, but they have not been brought to a common focus. Association technique with its place in experimental psychology and in the psychology of thinking and perception has developed concomitantly with projective method. The current derivatives of these two trends must be brought into alignment if we are to profit fully from both.

In the use of projective techniques generally, language has been tolerated as a necessary but often deceptive component. If projective inference itself is valid then language—the basic everyday medium of communication—ought to be able to furnish the necessary data from which inference is drawn.

Professional students of psychology have not heretofore had access to projective method and material which is likely to be meaningful at a relatively early stage in their professional careers. It has been apparent almost from the outset of our work that the sentence completion can be helpful in this respect.

Clinical psychologists and physicians who are otherwise skilled have often been deprived of the values of projective material because they have not had the long technical training which is generally required for mastery of projective method. Valid interpretation of the sentence completion is easily demonstrable by sympathetic, empathic, experienced clinicians with a minimum of technical training.

Finally, sentence completion lends itself to interpretation in simple, clear, descriptive language. This means not only that personality descriptions based on sentence completion records tend to be easy to read and to understand. It means also that the relative absence of ambiguity can make it readily possible for the interpretations by a particular examiner of a particular sentence completion record to be checked against external criteria. Thus, its use establishes grounds for needed caution in too hasty interpretation of projective data and quickly discourages efforts at premature objectification.

Toward all of these goals we believe the sentence completion, used in the ways which have been discussed in this book, can make substantial contribution.

Appendix

SENTENCE COMPLETION

Miale-Holsopple

INSTRUCTIONS

COMPLETE EACH SENTENCE in whatever way you wish. If you have trouble thinking of a completion to any sentence, put a circle around the number, and return to the sentence when you have finished the rest.

1. Children are usually certain that
2. People are praised when
3. A large crowd
4. A person is most helpless when
5. When an animal is wild
6. The hardest decisions
7. The easiest way to get money
8. Twenty years from now
9. Parents would worry less if
10. When fire starts
11. Compared with dogs, cats are
12. Fathers should learn that
13. One's closest friends can
14. It is easy to get into trouble when
15. Few children fear
16. At the end of the road
17. He drew back from the touch of
18. The white girl who married the colored man
19. The most pleasant dreams
20. A drunken man
21. No one can repair the damage caused by

(175)

22. The nicest thing about being a child
23. There is hardly any
24. To be without shame
25. Worse than being lonely is
26. When a person is ill
27. A man can stop beating his wife only if
28. The best thing about old age
29. Children are most annoying when
30. If people only knew how much
31. The main difference between a wild and a tame animal is
32. Few things are less attractive than
33. The worst thing about being sick
34. It is often hard to sleep when
35. People shouldn't
36. To be a good liar one must
37. A masculine woman should
38. People refrain from murder only because
39. Too much distance lies between
40. The best of mothers may forget that
41. There ought to be a law to
42. Spiders are
43. When a criminal leaves the prison he
44. Compared with sisters brothers are
45. The finger pointed
46. Children are least annoying when
47. To avoid a fight one must
48. A naked man
49. Closer and closer there comes
50. There would be more divorces if
51. A drunken woman
52. When a person is wounded
53. One's best friend may be irritating when
54. A woman's body

55. A weak person does not often
56. Down underground
57. One can hardly see
58. Wouldn't it be really funny if
59. The kind of animal I would like most to be
60. Nothing is harder to stop than
61. The two most beautiful things I have ever seen
62. She couldn't bear to touch
63. A woman who has lost her virtue must
64. Failure may be expected when
65. An effeminate man may
66. It hurts when
67. The deeper one goes
68. Behind one's back
69. When the car skidded
70. A mother is more likely than a father to
71. The worst kind of criminal
72. If one cannot own
73. Tests like this

Name .... Date ....Examiner..........

Sex .... Age .... Occupation ....

This Book

SENTENCE COMPLETION

By JAMES QUINTER HOLSOPPLE *and* FLORENCE R. MIALE

*was set, printed and bound by the E. W. Stephens
Publishing Company of Columbia, Missouri. The page
trim size is 5½x8½ inches. The type page is 23x39 picas.
The type face is Caledonia, set 11 point on 13 point.
The text paper is 60-pound Mountie Eggshell. The
cover is Holliston's Roxite LS Vellum 5175, 11M, two-
tone, Black.*

With THOMAS BOOKS *careful attention is given to
all details of manufacturing and design. It is the Publisher's desire to present books that are satisfactory as
to their physical qualities and artistic possibilities and
appropriate for their particular use.* THOMAS BOOKS
*will be true to those laws of quality that assure a good
name and good will.*

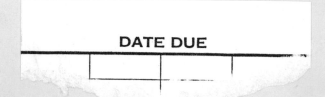

DATE DUE